Living Abundantly on Limited Assets

Anton Tkachenko

ISBN: 9781689010665

Dedicated to my parents.
Each inspired my pursuit of minimalism in their own special ways.

Contents

Chapter 1: Escaping Nuclear Disaster And Pursuing A Better Life In America

I was born in Ukraine in 1985. The Chernobyl disaster occurred in 1986. Shortly after the worst nuclear accident in history, my family decided to emigrate to America. We finally managed to leave the radioactive region shortly before the Berlin Wall fell around 1990.

Fast forward to late 2014. At age twenty nine, I found myself in my birth country of Ukraine in the depths of winter. After traveling around the world for several months, I eventually ran low on cash and tried to find a job in the capital city of Kiev. Ukraine was experiencing an armed conflict with Russia on its border. I left Ukraine as a child due to one nightmare and now I was back during another. A friend helped me land a gig writing articles about corruption and the armed conflict for an English language newspaper. Since my undergraduate thesis for my economics major was about the impact of corruption on Foreign Direct Investment, I thought it would feel good to use my academic interests to help my birth country by informing Western audiences of the situation. The pay would be about $500 a month. In a country where the average salary was a hundred or two less than that, I would have managed to live just fine. Sure, I ate a lot of beets and buckwheat to live on a few dollars a day but I was happy to be living with my cousin and near other family members as well as experiencing my roots. Unfortunately, I had a student loan, car payment, and car insurance back home in the US that was about five hundred dollars a month in total. Therefore, I was unable to take the job and had to come back to America. Forgoing this opportunity that I perceived as adventurous and Hemingway-esque was the catalyst that inspired me to become debt-free. I wanted to be able to take advantage of such rare opportunities in the future if they presented themselves.

A few months after returning to the US from Ukraine, I moved to downtown Los Angeles (DTLA). Armed with a new mission, I decided my two goals for life in LA were to pay off the remaining $20,000 of student loans as quickly as possible and to get rid of my car. I figured, adopting a car-free lifestyle would allow me to pay off college debt faster. I was keen to get rid of the loan quickly because it took nine years to pay the first twenty thousand dollars out of the $40k total I had after graduation. In addition, I reasoned that ditching personal car ownership would be good for the environment because LA was already known as one of the most polluted and traffic congested cities in the US.

I moved to Los Angeles in May 2015, sold my car in August 2015, and paid off the college loan in April 2016. At that point I was officially debt-free. Was it worth making the sacrifices and lifestyle changes described in this book in order to pay off half of my college debt in one year? Unequivocally, yes.

When I was a small child my parents wanted to leave Ukraine to come to America to pursue a better life. Eventually, around age thirty I interpreted that to mean a life without debt so that I could take opportunities that came my way even if they did not pay much. I wanted to live a life that was interesting, even if it was not necessarily a rich one. Ironically, a trip back to the Motherland inspired this personal definition of a "better life."

My goal to pay off the remainder of my college debt as quickly as possibly led to embracing minimalism. As part of this new lifestyle choice, I made it a mission to experience as much American culture as I could in Los Angeles for as cheap as possible. I began to see how abundant life could be even when living on limited assets. Unexpectedly, I realized how letting go of attachments to material possessions led to helping me let go of non-material things when life became complicated.

Chapter 2: Journey To America And Catching The Travel Bug

After running away from Ukraine, our family traveled to Vienna by train and stayed there for about a month. Afterwards, we lived near Rome for a few months. We gave up Ukrainian citizenship to come to America. While waiting for permission to fly to the United States, we lived with other refugees. We settled in Sioux Falls. After about a year in South Dakota, we took a bus to San Diego, California and made that home.

My childhood in San Diego began with an assimilation phase. Other than a few minor differences compared to good ol' Americans born in the USA, I was like many other boys by the time I was in middle school. I had friends, wanted to be liked, and I wanted to wear trendy clothes. At sixteen I got a new entry level car. I worked weekends and summers to pay car bills. For the most part, I was a somewhat average American during those middle school and high school years. I was well assimilated into this capitalist society.

Before the age of five I traveled extensively. Perhaps these adventures, even though I cannot remember many of them, inspired a love of travel. Then during elementary school years I spent a summer in Colorado. During middle school years I spent one summer in Seattle, and another summer in Ukraine. That summer was my first time back to the homeland since leaving the country.

During high school I wanted to get away from San Diego and attend college somewhere on the other side of the country. The thought of attending a small college with intimate class sizes and a sense of community was appealing. My high school counselor recommended I check out the College of Wooster. During a campus visit, there was a feeling in my stomach that solidified my decision to attend this school. After four years at this institute of higher learning, I am proud to call that experience one of the quintessentially "best years of my life."

Due to the Scottish heritage of the college, we had a bagpipe marching band that played at many campus events. I still have fond memories of waking up to live bagpipe music on some weekends whenever I hear this instrument in a movie or a song. The school was in the middle of corn fields in rural Ohio. I remember the surprise I experienced the first time I saw Amish people driving a horse and buggy down the main street that cut the campus in half. I was unaware of ever learning about Amish in the public schools of San Diego. It filled me with wonder about alternative lifestyles when I periodically saw Amish pass by campus. They seemed like true minimalists.

Since the school was relatively isolated from major population centers and almost all students were required to live on campus, the strong sense of community fostered by the college had a profound impact on my educational experience. I made some of the best friends I ever had in life. You develop deep bonds with people when you live in the same dorm as them, eat every dinner with them, study for the same class with them, take road trips to various places around the country with them, and enjoy all the other typical college shenanigans with them. These friends from different countries around the world became like brothers and one even became my college sweetheart. There were even memorable college traditions that we participated in, such as filling the nearly fifteen foot arch of the main classroom building with snow to block the doors because legend had it that doing so would result in canceled classes the next day. That epic night was like a huge party with several hundred students participating in good clean fun. Last but not least, the College of Wooster had one very special attribute - each graduating student was required to spend both semesters of their senior year working one-on-one with a professor in their major on an Independent Study thesis. My project ended up being nearly one hundred pages. Perhaps completing this massive undertaking during college gave me the courage to write a full length book.

After graduating college, I returned to San Diego and entered the "White Collar" workforce. I was the first in my family to graduate college and get a "Professional" job. After a few years I wanted to travel for work so I used my experience in financial services to land a job as a Branch Examiner. This role required auditing financial advisors to ensure their business practices were in compliance with investment industry regulations. The greatest benefit about the travel job was seeing new places and meeting diverse people. I moved to Austin, Texas for the new role. However, before starting the job I went on my first solo trip to Europe. The journey was about a month long. I traveled to Denmark, Germany, Holland, Belgium, France, and the UK.

The Austin-based firm employed financial advisors all over the country. It was a dream come true. I was paid to travel, explore, and go on adventures - as long as I fulfilled my professional obligations. From Spring 2012 to Spring 2014 I worked this gig. I was on the road about every other week. Roughly one hundred airplanes a year. Countless layovers in Dallas since Austin did not have many direct flights to small faraway cities. During those two years, work travel took me to about thirty five states. Additionally, I would take vacations abroad. During those two years in Austin I took personal trips to Spain, Morocco, Hong Kong, Thailand, Singapore, Japan, Mexico, Canada, and Colombia.

After two years of living out of a suitcase, I yearned for experiences that were less "American" since I spent two years on an extensive road trip around the US. I decided to start a new life in Puerto Rico. I figured my financial knowledge could be useful there, I could learn Spanish, and experience a different culture. Life on the "Island of Enchantment" only lasted two months. I got mugged at gunpoint around 9 a.m. on a weekday about a block away from the granny flat that I was renting. During this encounter, I was permitted to donate my iPhone and wallet, which included my drivers license, credit card, and about twenty dollars, to this young entrepreneur. The pistol incident was the final straw. There were several surprises about living in this territory of the US that made it an undesirable place to reside. Shortly after I arrived in San Juan that summer of 2014 the government was on the brink of bankruptcy, which made conditions on the island and employment prospects worse.

Disappointed that my hopes for Puerto Rico did not go as planned, I debated next steps. Shortly after leaving this territory, I hit the road again. I traveled to Australia, New Zealand, United Arab Emirates, Turkey, Greece, Bulgaria, Romania, Moldova, Transnistria (not officially a "real" country), and on to Ukraine. I rested with family in Kiev for a while. Then I traveled to Czech Republic, Austria, Slovakia, Hungary, Malta, and Italy. Departing from Venice, I flew back to Ukraine. After two months on the Caribbean island and five months of international travel, I depleted my funds. My attempts at starting a new life had not come to fruition. I felt obliged to go back to my "old" life. So I flew back to San Diego.

During January 2015 I returned to America. I traveled to about thirty countries in less than three years and visited every continent except Antarctica. Cash poor and with bills to pay, I knew endless international travel would not be possible forever. I also wanted stability and a stable long term relationship. I yearned to stay put in one area for a while. Most of my life was spent wanting to learn about other cultures. I neglected a deep dive into learning about America and its culture, people, history, and land.

Even though I wanted to get off the road, I was apprehensive about settling down in one place. Most jobs only give three weeks of vacation that I could use for travel. But I spent the last few years traveling far and wide. Staying put would be difficult. I would need to quell the gypsy spirit. Despite staying grounded in one location, the lessons I learned allowed me to grow in ways that brief visits to cities around the globe could not provide.

And so began the next chapter - settling down in Los Angeles for a couple years. I explored the city and surrounding areas exhaustively. During this time I developed a greater appreciation for America and gratitude for the opportunity to live in this nation. LA was an excellent base for learning about my adopted country. Simultaneously, I spent these two years attempting to live simpler. I hoped that decreased dependence on material possessions would allow for less stress, more independence, and greater focus on aspects of life more important than physical objects.

Possibly the greatest benefit of traveling to thirty countries was gaining the perspective that most people in the world live without many American conveniences, yet many of them appear happy. This insight further empowered my pursuit of minimalism.

One other benefit of extensive traveling was the opportunity to have detailed conversations with people from all walks of life. During my business travels around dozens of states, I noticed that many of my conversations with strangers in various settings involved people's financial situations. I learned that many in America were unhappy with the amount of debt they had. On the other hand, while traveling internationally, I observed that whenever people learned that I was from California, many would talk about their dreams to visit or move to Los Angeles. It was these recurring themes from my discussions with folks around the US and the world that inspired this book about minimalism and LA. I wanted to paint a realistic picture of the sacrifices required to live in a financially responsible manner as well as to provide an unbiased account of life in Los Angeles.

Chapter 3: Reverse Culture Shock In The Land Of Plenty

Upon returning to San Diego during January 2015 I experienced reverse culture shock. While traveling the world, I lived out of one carry-on suitcase as well as one backpack for my laptop and a few other items. In most cities and countries I visited I stayed in hostels. A bed in a hostel dorm allowed me to be frugal enough to travel for months.

Now I was back at my mom's house. Broke, no job, living in my childhood room, and almost thirty. This situation did not boost my confidence. Adjusting back to life in America made these few weeks even more challenging.

During this time most of California was experiencing water shortages. I recall seeing a large city bus with a message across the side stating "California in a state of drought." This bus had hardly anyone in it - perhaps a passenger or two. I was unable to help but think how wasteful it is to wash these giant buses when a smaller vehicle would suffice for the majority of bus routes in San Diego County. During the two months I spent in Ukraine during winter 2014-5 I would often commute via public van shuttles. These micro-buses were so packed that I usually stood up during the ride and felt like I was in a can of sardines. The buses were so filthy outside as if they got washed only when it rained. Inside there was no heating in the passenger area. I have fond memories of traveling in these dirty micro-buses, squished with the other sardines, and seeing my own breath because the temperature was below freezing.

Now back in coastal America, back in the land of plenty. Here most objects are bigger and usually take more resources to maintain.

The second reverse culture shock that I would have to overcome was knowing English. I recently came back from spending a significant amount of time in countries where I did not understand what people were saying. So I could people watch and enjoy walks around crowded areas without having to understand what people were talking about. I did not realize how much of a blessing this was until I came back to America. Now all of a sudden when I walked past people... people on their phones... humans talking to one another... I was bombarded with communications that I completely understood. For a few weeks, I experienced much agony from hearing the small talk of the common American. I was dumbfounded to hear the issues that people complained about. We were in San Diego, the sun was shining, the air was clean, we were in the first world. But enough is never enough. It seemed that the common person could always find something to complain about. I just spent two months in Ukraine during winter while the country was experiencing an ongoing armed conflict with Russia. I could not understand how there was so much to complain about in San Diego. These feelings subsided after some weeks as I acclimated.

Further surprises came while I was showering. For some reason, the hot water never ran out. After several minutes, there was still hot water. I did not understand. After I shampooed my hair and washed my body with soap, was I supposed to stand here and enjoy this hot water? I was flabbergasted. I almost called out to my mom after I got out to ask if she knew there was unlimited hot water. I became accustomed to life in Ukraine during that formidable winter - with its three minutes worth of hot water in the shower before needing to wait another hour for the boiler to heat up another few minutes worth of wet warmth.

To get my mind off these annoyances of adjusting back to the wealthy western world, I focused on searching for a job and dating.

Chapter 4: Traveled The World, Ran Out Of Money, Took The First Job I Was Offered

I needed to find a job as soon as possible. It's never ideal for a child to return to a parent's empty nest - especially when the child is nearly thirty years old. So I applied for jobs in San Diego, and when I exhausted those options I applied to positions in LA and beyond. This was a sign of desperation since most people who grew up in San Diego would never leave such a pleasant place for a massive concrete jungle associated with the worst traffic and pollution in the country. But I needed to start living on my own again, so I did what I felt was necessary.

As I pondered dating, insecurity swept over me. I worried that no woman would date a broke twenty nine year old with no job and living at his mom's condo. Financially, I was not in a position to take women out to dinners and movies. Out of necessity, I convinced myself that the best I could do was to take a date out for some tea, or frozen yogurt, or for one drink and a walk. Fortunately, San Diego has mild climate year round so evening strolls near the beach are a budget-friendly way to get to know someone.

To my surprise, the women I met did not mind that I was unemployed or that I could not take them out to dinners and entertainment. I got the impression that because I was able to pursue my dream to complete a lengthy trip around the world and that I was actively job searching, that this was viewed as having potential. As long as I was nice and caring, my temporary hardships were not deal-breakers. These experiences led to the unraveling of my preconceived notions that only wealthy men could be successful at dating.

I started going steady with a young woman I met at yoga. Shortly after starting to date this fellow yogi, I had an interview via video conference with a company near Santa Barbara. This firm gave me a job offer without me ever meeting the folks there in person. A couple thousand dollars was offered for relocation since I was required to move from San Diego. It was the first offer I received so I accepted it.

During March 2015 I moved to Ventura - a small beach town an hour north of LA.

The cozy studio apartment I rented was on a quiet street a few blocks from downtown Ventura where the restaurants, bars, and shops were located. At about five hundred square feet it was more than enough for one person.

Commuting to work was exceptionally beautiful. There was hardly any traffic during peak periods, which made the drive convenient. Each way was a twenty minute drive along the coast on Highway 101.

Ventura was a cool little city. Patagonia, the environmentally friendly clothing company, had its headquarters near the downtown area. This brought young people and liberal attitudes. There were plenty of ethnic restaurants, some live music venues, and some cozy bars, including one that was in a historic mansion. This city was more affordable than ritzy Santa Barbara thirty miles north. Ventura was a clean and quiet town yet it was only seventy miles from DTLA which provided access to world class entertainment on the weekends if you so desired.

Patagonia offered free yoga at their headquarters one night a week. I tried it once. Much to my chagrin, the free yoga was in their clothing showroom. And like many free events, it was packed. So here we were… a bunch of granola smelling millennials along with our mats rolled out as we were packed into a clothing store. I noticed high-end yoga mats, which presumably increase the chances of reaching enlightenment. While performing various poses I noticed the clothing on the periphery of the retail showroom and was unable to help but stare at the large pictures of people climbing intense mountains in Patagonia gear. I could not get into enough of a zen state to let the following thought leave my mind: the clothing sold by this company is so expensive that by simply forgoing purchases of their attire, I may actually be able to save enough money to go visit some of these places pictured in these large photos on the wall. Sure, I would likely never be climbing those same mountains in the photos on the wall, but I could surely find some other moderate yet beautiful hikes in the Patagonia region of South America.

Wandering around Ventura, I saw a lot of people sporting Patagonia gear, as one sees folks in San Francisco Bay Area wearing North Face because it is headquartered there, and locals in Portland wearing Columbia because its primary corporate office is in that city. It is cool to support local. But I could not justify spending hard earned wages on expensive threads for everyday wear. I wondered how many adventures and hikes atop frigid mountains I could embark on if I avoided mountains of debt from pricey attire purchases. I did not return to free yoga at Patagonia after that initial visit. Nor have I purchased any clothing from the company till this day. But in the few years since that time I have ventured to picturesque landscapes, lakes, seas, glaciers, mountains, and meadows.

Another offering provided by living in Ventura was proximity to Ojai 15 miles away. This quaint village of a few thousand residents had boutique shops, mom and pop restaurants, wine bars, retreats, small hotels, and hiking trails. A feeling of country living and a sense of being surrounded by nature was the greatest aspect of visiting Ojai. Two hours from LA, Ojai was excellent for Angelenos seeking respite from the hustle and bustle and traffic and pollution. At the time of this writing, Ojai has become increasingly popular because there are not too many small towns within a weekend trip from LA that have such trendiness potential.

Santa Barbara was also within about half an hour from Ventura and made for great weekend day trips to wander around the beaches and streets of this historical Spanish mission town with a Mediterranean climate.

For even more adventure, there was also the must-see small town of Solvang about 60 miles from Ventura. This town is famous for Danish village architecture and windmills, Danish heritage, Danish foods such as pancake balls known as aebleskiver, and a plethora of nearby wineries.

To highlight another benefit of living in this area of the country, it is worth noting a question I was asked during the interview for the job in Santa Barbara County. A senior person at the firm asked me how I feel about living in this area. It was a legitimate question since my hometown was San Diego and I had not lived near Santa Barbara or even LA before. The person asking the question wanted to be sure I would enjoy living in a small town rather than somewhere like LA, which many younger folks in the region may prefer. I responded that while I was working in San Diego for a few years after college I fell in love with surfing and engaged in this activity almost daily. My surfing days lasted for a couple years until I moved to Austin. During this period in my life, I joined some friends on a surfing camping trip to Rincon Point in Santa Barbara County. I advised the interviewer that this was the best surfing I experienced in my life and that this particular beach was known to have some of the best waves in southern California. Not that I surfed for a large portion of my life or was an expert or traveled far and wide to catch waves, but I was able to ride waves fairly well. The waves at Rincon Point were the longest rides I ever surfed. Rincon Point was within a few miles of the office where I was interviewing. Eagerness was expressed over the potential to be able to surf at this break regularly instead of having to drive four hours from San Diego.

There was plenty to explore in the Ventura area. However, shortly after starting the job in Santa Barbara County, I learned about issues related to the new role that were less than clear during the brief interview. So even though I was grateful to live in a cool place like Ventura, have a great commute to work, and the job was not terribly stressful, I could not see myself there long term.

In the meantime, I began creating a budget and analyzing my spending.

Chapter 5: Learning To Budget And Cutting Out Middlemen By Cutting Out Processed Foods

The March 2015 job offer in Santa Barbara County was for $62,000 a year. Hardly a handsome sum for this pricey area.

After taxes, health insurance premiums, and a little into 401k, my monthly take home pay was about $3,100.

Budget estimates in Ventura, CA during March 2015 were:

Expenses	
Rent (utilities included):	$950
Car payment:	$330
Cell phone:	$100
Student loan:	$100
Car insurance:	$100
Internet:	$ 40
Gym:	$ 30
Food:	$500
Miscellaneous:	$100
Gas:	$200
Total monthly expenses:	$2,450
Leftover savings:	$3,100 - $2,450 = $650

$650 a month in savings was not a lot of money. At that rate I would have enough to take a two week vacation once a year to somewhere like Europe or Asia assuming I stayed in hostels. But saving up for a down payment on a house seemed out of the question.

Since I recently spent several months abroad I knew there were opportunities to work while traveling. But the pay was not much. There would be no additional income to cover student loan expenses back home in high American dollar amounts. Not wanting to miss such opportunities if I took another big international trip again made me keen to pay off my college loan.

More motivation to get out of college debt came when I noticed it took about a decade to pay back nearly $20,000 and I still owed another twenty grand. I did not want to spend another decade on this balance. I needed to get this burden off my shoulders. Besides, with about $20k left as of 2015 at 5% interest I was going to pay about one thousand dollars that year to the government and its contractors to basically do nothing. Then the following year I would pay a tad less than a grand. And on and on till I finally paid off the loan.

I pondered ways to improve my savings. Eating habits seemed like a natural starting point because I had control over this and could implement change immediately.

The best way to increase savings was to limit money spent at restaurants. Nightlife and drinks were drastically cut as well since I partied away plenty of money during my early twenties.

Lunches during the week consisted of food I would bring from home. Restaurant lunches even one day during the work week was out of the budget. I would bring fruits, nuts, and yogurt to work. Fearing boredom would arise if I ate the same fruits and nuts each day, I diversified the portfolio of fruits and nuts consumed each week. Trader Joe's grocery store had several varieties of nuts that came in individual packs of one type of nut per bag. As an added bonus, these were unsalted - which I found to be healthier for me. So I loaded up on each individual bag of nuts that the market offered: almonds, Brazil nuts, cashews, hazelnuts, macadamia nuts, peanuts, pecans, pine nuts, pistachios, pumpkin seeds, sunflower seeds, and walnuts. One pack of each of the above dozen nuts and seeds cost almost one hundred dollars total. Most of the packages were one pound. So I took a giant bag of little packages of nuts to work and left them in my drawer. All these nuts lasted about three months. Then I would go back to Trader Joe's to refill the stash in my office drawer. I liked to think I would get a variety of vitamins and minerals and avoid boredom if I ate twelve different varieties over the course of a few months rather than always sticking to a few favorites.

A similar strategy was applied to fruit selection. I figured a greater variety of fruit eaten over the course of a week resulted in more types of vitamins, minerals, and nutrients for my body. Every Sunday I stocked up on produce. I would purchase one of each type of fruit and one of each type of vegetable that I needed to last the week. In total there were about thirty five items of fresh produce purchased each week. One banana, one papaya, one Gala apple, one Pink Lady apple, one watermelon, one Asian pear, one bartlett pear, one tomato, one potato, one bell pepper, one bunch of spinach, one carrot, one avocado, and on and on and on.

Strategy for breakfast and lunch at work: Wake up, shower, dress, drive to work, have some decaf tea, eat nuts and fruits around 9 or 10 a.m. Around lunchtime take a walk or go sit in my car and rest for half an hour to take my eyes off the computer and my mind off work to recharge, especially since I never drink caffeine. Then a few hours later, have some different fruits and nuts. Usually about two servings of fruit and a cup of nuts two times a day.

Increasing the variety of food continued with grains and other complex carbs. Each night during the workweek, dinner was cooked at home and consisted of a grain prepared in the rice cooker, with a veggie or two or a form of animal protein - usually fish rather than meat. To hedge the risk that I would get bored of always eating rice, I went to Whole Foods and Trader Joe's and bought as many different grains as were available. These were rice, black wild rice, steel cut oats, quinoa, barley, faro, buckwheat, amaranth, millet, teff, and corn grits.

During the workweek one night of dinner consisted of a microwaved potato and a can of sardines in oil. While sardines aren't a favorite of most Americans, Europeans - especially those from Eastern Europe and the Baltics love them as much as US folks who gobble down canned tuna. Another weekly staple was one four ounce pack of smoked wild salmon and one avocado - this was enough for two nights worth of dinner when combined with a heaping of complex grains. That left two nights for complex carbs and a veggie or two - usually sauteed with olive oil. Eggs were kept around for the weekend to have for breakfast. That was a break from all the nuts eaten at the office during the workweek. Weekends were also for breaks from homemade dinners and abstinence from red meat. I tried to be conscientious of ethical and environmental concerns over animals as food but the cravings for red meat about once a week could not be resisted at this time. Even these splurges were on affordable meats such as BBQ ribs or brisket rather than pricey steakhouse visits.

I was able to trim down my monthly food costs and eat very healthy. In addition, these meals were easy and efficient to prepare and clean, which freed up time for daily gym sessions. Furthermore, the majority of my food purchases consisted of items that had as their ingredients only the one actual ingredient itself. In other words, I rarely consumed foods that were made with many ingredients such as chips, trail mix, TV dinners, pasta sauce or macaroni. The reason for this was simple - to limit costs, you need to limit how many people are involved in the chain. Each additional person and or refinement adds an additional cost. Someone back in San Diego told me there was a guy living in one of the beachfront mansions who made all his wealth by creating recipes for granola bars and trail mixes. Imagine earning millions over the years by deciding what percent of a trail mix is going to be peanuts compared to raisins compared to chocolate chips. While I never fact checked this particular tale, the narrative provided motivation to continue living smaller. Each time someone decides what percent of a packaged food product will be a certain ingredient, it is reasonable to assume that this person needs to be paid a salary or fee. There are also marketing costs, design costs, etc. To save money, it seems wise to limit dependence on middlemen. I often think about the marketing executives at food conglomerates who earn hundreds of thousands of dollars a year and have teams of professionals working on making their food products and labels look more appealing psychologically. I would rather avoid spending even a penny of my hard earned dollars on paying the salaries of these marketing and design professionals and food scientists. It is enough that the simple foods I purchase already have plenty of other costs built in - such as logistics, shipping, packaging, legal contracts, currency conversions, etc. So I derive joy in knowing that the dozen varieties of nuts at Trader Joe's are simply the house brand in plain packaging and there is no fancy MBA executive in Chicago who is tasked with making the packaging look sexy. I am getting the nuts for the nutrition - not because of catchy phrases or pretty pictures on the package. Same logic for the complex grains. And when I buy thirty five or so types of fruits and veggies at one unit of each item, there is certainly no fancy marketing on the one lone carrot that I purchase. This is another way to exercise independence while saving money.

I thought to myself: With all these numerous types of nuts, fruits, veggies, and complex carbs, I am essentially eating one giant multivitamin over the course of a week. This is not medical advice nor am I qualified to provide nutritional opinions.

Another budget friendly dietary habit was to press the juice out of lemons or limes, grate some fresh ginger, and mix them together with fresh mint leaves in a blender. This concoction was poured into an ice cube tray and frozen. In the morning, one of these solid cubes was placed in a cup of hot water. The elixir was a refreshing, caffeine-free way to start the day.

There are countless articles and opinions about health foods and so-called superfoods. I read about some of these but the sheer volume and range of opinions made the task daunting. However, it appeared that, in general, foods such as hemp seeds, flax seeds, and chia seeds were championed by the wellness community. Not wanting to miss out on all the supposed benefits I would buy a small pack of each of these three esteemed health foods and would shake them up together in one container. I would now have what I called a Mega Omega Power Mix. I ate a spoon full of this mix daily. After several months I failed to observe any noticeable impact on my health. I discontinued consuming said Mega Omega Power Mix. The point was, I was experimenting and trying to be proactive with preventative healthcare. You don’t always get recipes right. Tastes and habits evolve over time. There is no lifelong recipe for success. It is important to periodically reevaluate systems.

Chapter 6: Can I Bike To Work? And The Cost Of Car Ownership

When I moved back to San Diego after college there were times I would bicycle to work instead of driving. The bike commute from downtown to near La Jolla was fifteen miles each way. Fortunately, there was a shower at the office. Cycling to work during chilly mornings was a great way to wake up. Riding back was a healthy outlet for stress relief after a long day of working on the computer.

During my time in Ventura the drive from home to the office was fifteen miles. I pondered commuting to work by bicycle again as I did in San Diego a few years before. The difference was that in San Diego I owned a car as a backup plan for days when I might not feel well enough to bike an hour to work or the weather was unfavorable. Since Ventura was about four hours north of San Diego by car, the weather was much more chilly. And there was no legitimate mode of public transport from where I lived to where I worked. So, if I got rid of my car and was too sick to bike or it was raining, I would be in a bind.

While considering cycling to work, I Googled around to research how many miles the average bicycle commuter rides each day. Fifteen miles each way seemed too long of a daily commute given I would have no backup plan.

So I took a look at my car, which I loved. It was the auto I dreamed of having. Small and compact yet fun. Manual transmission because I enjoyed stick shift ever since I began driving in my teens. Like many Americans, I had personal memories attached to my car. My family and I were in a similar model during my childhood when we went on an exhilarating road trip to a volcano in Washington state. The hatchback reminded me of a car I had in high school, which brought a growing sense of independence and upcoming manhood. There were many emotions attached to this material object. I did not want to let go of these attachments. However, I needed to get my savings up. So I convinced myself that I would still have these memories and emotions even if I parted ways with this automobile.

The more budget friendly alternative I came up with was to sell my car that was costing me $330 a month and lease a small, fuel-efficient hybrid Toyota Prius C for about $200 a month. This smaller car, I presumed, would also cost less to insure and could possibly cut my monthly gas expense in half to $100 a month.

Thinking of selling a car that I loved to increase my savings by $200 a month did not seem worthwhile. But I knew this was a process of unwinding my attachments to material possessions and starting to become financially prudent.

Before executing the plan to sell the fun car for a practical petro sipper, an unexpected event occurred.

Chapter 7: Moving To The Guatemalan Neighborhood

In April I received a call from a financial services firm in LA to which I applied after I arrived back to the US in January 2015. I already worked at the Santa Barbara County firm for a couple weeks. The LA firm scheduled an in-person interview. Before the interview I was worried they would be concerned about the one year gap in my resume. I felt obliged to explain that I spent part of that time job searching and another part traveling the world. The future supervisor did not appear to care one bit. In fact, her responses suggested that the travels were a positive aspect.

The offer letter stipulated a better title by one level. But more importantly, the pay was $80,000 a year, which was much more than the $62,000 I was earning near Santa Barbara. I started at this LA firm in June 2015.

I moved to downtown Los Angeles in May 2015. I wanted to live close to work so I could walk or take a short ride on the public transit. Now I would be able to get rid of my car. The additional salary would also allow me to pay off the remainder of my student loan quicker.

The new position was in the Capital Markets department of an investment bank. Since college I dreamed of working at an investment bank because it seemed exciting and lucrative. My role would be on the compliance side so I would not be earning as much as an analyst in one of the three main functions of an investment bank (Trading, Research, or Investment Banking). However, I would work on a team that supervised these functions and I would learn about those departments. On the plus side, working in compliance would be less hours than the three core departments.

I never thought I would live in the core of an urban area that was synonymous with traffic and pollution. But the significant salary, dream to live car-free, and the opportunity to work with the exciting areas of an investment bank were too much to resist.

I even derived joy from the prospect of working in a fancy high-rise building in the Financial District with the company's name on the top of the structure. This hedonistic delight derived from superficial status symbols was quite 'fake.' In retrospect, I am surprised that I was preoccupied with such pretentious matters.

The thought of another move and job transition was stressful. I recently traveled around the world for months, moved back to San Diego, and two months later moved to Ventura. Two months after moving to Ventura I moved to DTLA. However, all these moves were a good opportunity to get rid of material possessions that were not absolutely necessary. Having minimal possessions allowed me to be nimble and take advantage of this opportunity in LA.

The furniture I possessed included a queen size bed with black wood frame and a small dining room table with two chairs that matched the color and material of the bed frame. These items were purchased from IKEA with the relocation funds provided by the job that got me to Ventura. Prior to that I was traveling so I did not own much more than clothes and a laptop. The only other piece of "furniture" I owned in Ventura was an inexpensive foldable royal blue beach chair, which cost about ten dollars.

Since I hardly owned much furniture or belongings I searched for a studio apartment, which would cost several hundred dollars less per month compared to a one bedroom. I saw luxurious amenities as a waste of cash. Therefore, I opted to find an apartment in an older building rather than some fancy "loft" or whatever developers were calling these residences to convince yuppies to spend more on rent.

I looked at one apartment that seemed ok but it was much closer to Koreatown than downtown so the search continued. The next apartment was a few blocks from the Rampart station of the LA Police Department - of the notorious Rampart scandal in the late 1990s, which exposed widespread police corruption in the anti-gang division. Judging by the plethora of gang graffiti it appeared that the street where the apartment was located may have had active gang violence. A makeshift memorial for a young adult that was recently murdered was on the sidewalk in front of the apartment building that I came to see. My gut told me that did not feel comfortable. That particular street lacked the coziness for which I hoped. Search continued. I found a nice studio in an older building that was seven blocks from work - the closest of all the places I viewed up to that point. The inside of the apartment unit was nice and was recently remodeled. Apartment manager seemed affable and about my age. Neighborhood was less than ideal due to ubiquitous graffiti, trash on the streets and sidewalk, and proximity to a main road with a steady stream of vagrants, but appeared a bit more habitable than the previous one; so it would suffice.

Chapter 8: Rags To Riches On My Walk To Work

So began the next chapter of my life: Working with some of the wealthiest residents of LA, while residing among some of the poorest citizens in the City of Angels. On each morning's walk to work I passed people covered in rags, then worked with folks covered in riches.

Many jobs come with surprises. Some employers will leave out details that could potentially paint the position in an unsavory light. Not mentioned during the interviews was that I would have to be in the office no later than 6:30 a.m. each day. Stock market trading hours began at 9:30 a.m. on the East Coast and I was required to be in my seat on the institutional trading desk by that time. Prior to this job, I believe the earliest I arrived at work was 8 a.m. There was a bit of an adjustment period. Getting used to these hours was annoying at first but not a deal breaker. On the bright side, I got out at 3:30 p.m. and could go to the gym pool before the lap lanes got congested with LA traffic.

The second unexpected requirement of the job was having to wear a tie every day except for Fridays. This was a surprise since I never held a job where a tie was necessary, especially because as an in-house compliance person you almost never interact with clients face to face. LA gets hot in the summer and it's quite warm most of the year so the tie seemed like an unnecessary headache. I did what was required.

Employer's office was in the Financial District and adjacent to the I-110 freeway. Walking seven blocks from my apartment to work took about ten minutes. When leaving work to go home the first two blocks were fine because there was a local government agency occupying a large building. However, with each successive block west towards my apartment there would be progressively more trash on the sidewalks and more destitute people. Each morning, lunch break, and afternoon I walking around one of the poorest areas of LA while wearing slacks, a long sleeve button shirt, and a necktie. It felt a bit uncomfortable, especially since I hardly ever saw anyone else in this area wearing a necktie.

After two years of walking around a poverty stricken neighborhood while wearing a fancy necktie and a white collar outfit, my worries based on one mugging in Puerto Rico proved unwarranted. Not a single individual tried to rob me in LA. Nor did anyone try to inflict any physical harm upon me or genuinely pursue a bona fide altercation. It is possible that my initial outlook would have been a bit more rosy if I never poked around the LAPD's Crime Mapping website shortly after moving to DTLA. The site displayed a detailed record of criminal incidents, including location, date, and descriptions such as robbery, assault, exhibiting deadly weapon, motor vehicle theft, petty theft, theft from vehicle, spousal abuse - aggravated assault, assault with a deadly weapon, and burglary. Crime stats found on the public site were startling because they showed the countless unlawful acts which were occuring in my immediate neighborhood on a regular basis. Initial alarm over the amount of shady happenings in the vicinity of my new residence resulted in my neglecting to consider these events on a per capita basis. It is likely that on a per capita basis the quantity of crimes was less staggering. In my reaction to such negative news on the crime stats site, I forgot one of the cardinal rules regarding street smarts: one can greatly improve their odds of staying out of trouble if they do their best to keep a low profile and avoid starting any issues with other people.

Chapter 9: Walden 2.0

Despite the poverty surrounding my apartment building I was content that I found such a bargain for $995 a month. Since the building was nearly a century in age, the water, heating, and electricity were included in the rent. There was a security gate at the front entrance which required either a key or a code. Inside the unit was clean and when in my home a few floors up I could not see all the filth and intriguing characters. Upon walking into the apartment there was a hallway that led to the living space. Before arriving in the bedroom you first passed a bathroom on the right then a small kitchen that included a conventional size fridge and oven. Recent remodeling furnished the kitchen with new cabinets and modern countertops as well as pretty albeit fake wood flooring. After passing the kitchen you walk into the space that was about the size of an average American bedroom. That was it. The queen size bed and frame in one corner took about one third of the floor space in the bedroom/living area. A small wooden dining table with two chairs was in another corner and a small coffee table in a third corner. It would have been nice to have another fifty square feet, which would have created space for a small two seater couch. Royal blue foldable beach chair sat low to the ground near my bed; this was my temporary-turned-two-year substitute for a couch and is where I ate most of my dinners. As a bonus: a large window in the bedroom and kitchen faced east to a beautiful view of the skyscrapers.

In total, the space was about three hundred and fifty square feet. Most white collar professionals outside of New York City or San Francisco would likely find life in such a small space unfathomable. This was certainly the smallest apartment I have ever lived in. Fortunately, I lived in dorm rooms all four years of college. In addition, I have lived in many tight living quarters while bouncing around hostels. These two experiences helped me realize that humans do not need as much space as the status quo suggests. Nonetheless, to cope with the feeling of living in a tiny space, I thought about my desire to travel around the US in a motorhome and how living here would be great preparation for such a trip.

My compact apartment reminded me of the two primary goals I set for myself upon returning from world travels. Firstly, to pursue a smaller and simpler life to focus on joys beyond material possessions and to pay off my student loan. The second objective was to learn to appreciate my adopted country of America and its culture rather than solely looking beyond our borders for fascination and intrigue by exotic cultures. With both of these goals in mind, I read *Walden* by Henry David Thoreau. Completing this book was one of the first times I explored great American literature as a source of motivation for my personal life.

First published in 1854, *Walden* was about the two years that Thoreau spent living in a small ten by fifteen foot cabin at Walden Pond in Massachusetts. The book's core themes are simple living, self-reliance, and spiritual growth. I began reading the novel a few months after moving into my 'urban cabin' in LA, which was about twice the size of Thoreau's. The book provided guidance on overcoming the challenges associated with a shift to a simpler life. In one exceptionally memorable passage, Thoreau ponders what he could do for a living and writes that he does not need to work much because his greatest skill is not wanting much. Elsewhere, the author writes that working six weeks a year was sufficient for a year of living expenses. Thoreau's *Walden* was inspiring.

DTLA was grungy and the streets were covered with litter. The apartment building where I resided was quite old. When living in such conditions, there are times when you have unexpected visitors. October 2015 brought a first such visitor - a giant cockroach the length of a conventional door key. Whenever such guests arrived I would help facilitate their passage into heaven. Fortunately, such visits did not occur on more than a handful occasions per year. My reading of *Walden* could hardly be more timely. Thoreau mentioned his cabin was settled by numerous wasps but they did not bother him much and, in fact, he felt a sense of joy that these insects found his home so hospitable. For me personally, I did not mind seeing and killing an occasional roach. However, I was worried that a day I had a woman over, a roach would decide that that would be an ideal time to present itself. In addition, when one upgrades their standard of living it is much more difficult to go back to a humbler residence after becoming accustomed to a more glamorous apartment. I wanted to avoid this so I could be more flexible in the future.

To summarize, living conditions could be much worse. I recall staying the night in the living room of a friend's apartment in Brooklyn a few years before. There was a rodent that woke me from my slumber. At least my DTLA apartment did not have such sizeable roommates. I could have gotten a nicer apartment in a fancy building, but I was essentially saving several thousand dollars a year to kill a dozen roaches. A few thousand dollars a year is a significant amount to put towards paying off debt or into a retirement fund. Alternatively, such a sum could bless me with a marvelous vacation for a couple weeks. The positive experiences from such a trip would far outweigh having to squish a bug on occasion.

Aside from minor annoyances discussed above, the only difference between the inside of my apartment and most average apartments was the lack of air conditioning, a garbage disposal in the kitchen sink, and a dishwasher.

Since electricity was included in the rent, I could have purchased a portable indoor air conditioning unit for a few hundred dollars but I opted not to that first summer in LA. In retrospect, I do not know how I survived summer 2015 without AC in the apartment. A year later in June 2016 I caved and purchased an AC unit for $350. This was not a very minimalist life choice, but I lived a year without one and June 2016 brought the first 100 degree day. Such heat was worsened by the fact that the building I lived in was made of brick and extremely old. Heat would be trapped inside making the indoor temperature hotter than outside. I noticed my performance and concentration at work were severely declining due to lack of rest. I was only able to sleep four or five hours a night in such hellish heat. Deciding to purchase this materialist good was out of necessity rather than desire for convenience.

Lack of a garbage disposal in the kitchen sink was expected. I lived in old buildings in San Diego and Ventura where I experienced this slight inconvenience before. Overcoming this challenge simply requires getting a new kitchen sink strainer and pouring a bottle of Drano clog remover down the pipe every couple months.

My tiny urban cabin also lacked a dishwater, as have a few other places where I lived. As a child, we never used a dishwasher. I grew up having to wash dishes by hand on a regular basis. So I was used to this and okay with a bit of manual work rather than relying on a machine.

Rental expense did not include a dedicated parking spot so I relied on street parking. Parking was extremely difficult in this area because of the proximity to DTLA. Aside from difficulty in finding a parking spot for my car, the situation was more annoying because once a week there was street cleaning so I would have to move my car to another place during my lunch break then move it back after work. It seemed that most people who owned cars in this neighborhood did not commute to work with them since most of the spots on the streets were taken at all times of the day.

However, I planned to begin a car-free life and expected I would not need to deal with the hassles of LA parking for much longer. At the end of August 2015 I finally sold my car. I continued living without personal car ownership for the remainder of the two years spent in LA.

Chapter 10: Learning To Live On Half Of My After-Tax Income

It took time to adjust to the poor conditions around my new residence. Living in DTLA was the first time I resided around so much filth. However, I was grateful for the money I saved. During summer 2015 DTLA was beginning to gentrify rapidly. Whole Foods, the nationwide health food chain, held its grand opening in the center of DTLA on November 4, 2015. This was a game changer. Prior to Whole Foods opening in this area, there was no health food supermarket anywhere near downtown. Whole Foods gave their blessing to downtown; it was now okay for the hipsters and yuppies to live here without feeling ashamed. For brief historical context, LA was different compared to most cities in the sense that downtown offered almost zero fine dining, nightlife, and entertainment for well-off folks until this time. I was told that for decades, people who worked in DTLA would rush to their cars as soon as their shift was over to get on the road before dark in order to avoid trouble. When Staples Center sports arena opened in 1999 urban conditions began to improve and downtown became somewhat habitable for white collar professionals. It took another decade or more before this change gained enough momentum for crime to come down to tolerable levels, and yuppies and hipsters thought it okay to live in the area.

When I moved to DTLA in summer 2015 there were some nice apartments near my office that were suitable for white collar types and other professionals, but not many. These white collar friendly apartments were about $2,000 a month for a studio. According to my research, the cheapest monthly rent for one of these nicer places was about $1,800, which did not include water, heat, and electricity so would have been close to two grand after utilities. Some of these higher end apartments were as far of a walk to work as the place I chose, which cost $1,000 and included all utilities except internet. As an added benefit I was not required to have rental insurance as an extra expense to live in this old building. I did not want to pay double the rent to live in a tall building with a nice lobby, modern amenities, and a sexy name.

It was settled. I did not need to feel bad about the cons of my living situation because the pros were that I was saving a good chunk of change. If I was paying $1,000 for my housing and others were paying double, I should be on track to save more than ten thousand dollars a year. Since I partied my surplus earnings away during my early twenties and traveled with my excess funds during my late twenties, I needed to pay off my debt and step up retirement fund contributions.

Knowing the approximate amount spent on traveling the world during 2014-5, I figured ten thousand dollars could support about six months of traveling if I went to poor European countries, South East Asia, or parts of Latin America. In most of these countries you can get a bed in a hostel for about ten dollars a night. Or if staying longer term, it may be possible to find a room in an apartment to rent for a month at about the same nightly rent.

Ultimately, my top priority was paying off my education loan and thereby becoming entirely debt free. The second goal was possibly taking another sabbatical to travel the world for several months. Motivation for these two objectives was so strong that the small inconveniences of living in a cheap apartment was well worth it. Besides, even though the apartment building was in a poorer area a few blocks from the financial district, there was less foot traffic and car traffic so I presumed life would be a tad less chaotic than if I lived in the very center of the city.

Monthly budget estimates for life in downtown Los Angeles after I sold my automobile in August 2015:

After tax take home pay:	$4,390
Expenses	
Rent:	$1,000
Cell phone:	$85
Education loan:	$100
Internet:	$30
Gym:	$50
Food:	$350
Miscellaneous:	$50
Total expenditures:	$1,665

Savings in this budget estimate: $4,390 - $1,665 = $2,725.

The actual savings were a bit less than estimates because I used funds for local adventures and exploring. However, such activities were done as cost effectively as possible.

The planned savings for this new life in LA was approximately four times the amount compared to life in Ventura, CA. I would, in theory, be able to pay off my college loan four times faster than if I never left the quaint coastal town for the rough concrete jungle.

Now that I began my adjustment to living a simpler life, it was time to begin my pursuit of learning to appreciate what life in America offered. Time to start practicing gratitude for this place and in this moment. Time to enjoy the bountiful experiences within reach rather than traveling to far away lands.

Chapter 11: Living Next To A Rooster To Pay Off Student Debt From The College Of Wooster

I lived seven blocks west of the Financial District in DTLA. My apartment was about two miles from Little Tokyo, two and a half miles from Chinatown, one and a half miles from Historic Filipinotown, two miles from Koreatown, four and a half miles from Thai Town and Little Armenia, two miles from the El Salvador Community Corridor, and six miles from Little Ethiopia. Lastly, about half a mile from my abode was an area that appeared to have a large concentration of Guatemalan establishments. There were signs in the Guatemalan area that stated "Se Habla Quiché." I knew that Se Habla Espanol meant 'Spanish is spoken' but I had zero clue what Quiché was. It turns out that Quiché (alternatively spelled K'iche') is one of the Mayan languages spoken by an indigenous group in Guatemala. It was interesting to learn that there were Mayan languages spoken in my neighborhood. However, there was no official designation like Little Guatemala by the city at the time.

I was excited to start living here because it felt like I was in the middle of the world. There were many foreign cultures in close proximity. I would get to learn more about these cultures, eat their authentic cuisine, and meet diverse people; all while living in America and simultaneously learning about and experiencing American culture.

However, in America there is a saying: "There is no such thing as a free lunch." In return for walkable proximity to work and gym, saving a large portion of my income, living within a few miles of countless cultural amenities - both foreign and American, I had to pay. Rather than monetary, the payment came in the form of having to tolerate numerous unpleasantries.

The most surprising problem of my new living situation in DTLA was my neighbor - a rooster. My apartment at the end of the building was closest to the backyard of the house on the other street. This house was converted into a multi-unit dwelling. Residents of one of the units in the house owned a rooster and chickens, which lived in the side yard. The cock would crow every morning at about 5:00 a.m.

Work required that I be in the office no later than 6:30 a.m. so I did not mind if the rooster would crow at 5:30 a.m. when I would get up anyway. But on most days the cockerel would commence its wake up screeching before my alarm clock went off. Having sleep disturbed and waking up a half hour early on occasion is one thing but it is deeply frustrating when this occurs everyday for an extended period of time. I was extremely surprised that living in the downtown of a wealthy and developed city would require me to have a feathered foe as a neighbor. Prior to this scenario, I always associated such animals with the countryside.

About two weeks after I moved in and started the new job, my sisters came up from San Diego to visit me during June 2015. The next day they woke up and walked to the 7-Eleven two blocks from my apartment. On their way there they saw the rooster walking with one of the female chickens towards the 7-Eleven. Once we were ready to start our day we drove to the street parallel to where I was living to see if we could spot that cock with his chicken girlfriend. At 9:30 a.m. the rooster, with its red head, brown feathered upper body and black feathered lower body, was crossing the residential street in front of the house where it lived. The fact that this was a few blocks from the financial district of the second largest city in America continues to puzzle me.

The rooster situation would continue to be a form of tax that I would have to pay via my pain. Instead of only complaining about it I intended to take action. I called the LA Animal Shelter. They said chickens were allowed but roosters were not allowed in the city if there is another residence adjacent to where the cockerel lives. Eventually someone from the shelter came by to look for the cock. When I called back they said they did not see it. The animal shelter told me that in order for them to send a letter warning the owners that roosters were prohibited by city ordinance I would need to find out who owns it. I told them that the house has been converted to a multi-family dwelling and there was no way to tell what the unit numbers were since the house only had one address number on it but no apartment numbers. They responded that that was not their concern.

I strolled down the filth covered sidewalk in the impoverished neighborhood in attempts to find out who owned the rooster. I saw a little boy playing out front of the shabby house that had been converted into a multi-unit dwelling. The kid appeared about six years old. I asked if he knew who owned the animal. The boy innocently responded it was his family's. I inquired if he could take me to his parents. As I walked through the front door of the building and into the hallway inside, I grew nervous about the residents perceiving my request as criticism of their lifestyle choices or as being imposing. The little boy took me to his apartment which was near the front door of the house. His mom came to the door. I asked her if she could get rid of the foul fowl because it was clearly bothering many of the neighbors. She said no because the rooster was part of the family. The mother quickly shooed me away. I was unable to find out the apartment number while talking to the woman because it was not clearly marked. And, thus, my animal adversary continued to crow for the two years while I resided near it.

Next door to Rooster House was a home with a German shepherd. Similarly, the place where the dog lived was a big house that was converted to a multi-family dwelling. Yet again, it was impossible to know which unit housed the owner of this dog. I did not feel comfortable trying to make friends with the people who lived in these houses just to find out who owned the shepherd.

This German shepherd barked all day; not only at sunrise and throughout the morning like the cock next door. It was so sad. I felt worse for the dog than I felt for myself having to hear the dog barking all day. It was scrawny and looked ill. Not once in two years did I see an owner play with it or pet it or take it for a walk. On only a couple of occasions did I even see a human go near the dog - and that was usually just to get around it. Yes, my apartment offered me a beautiful view of the downtown skyline, but I also overlooked a full view of the backyard of the house where the German shepherd lived. It was heartbreaking to see this animal be so neglected. Perhaps the dog was simply used to keep criminals from coming near the property. I thought people got dogs for companionship; which was definitely not the case here.

And, of course, for selfish reasons, it pained me to experience constant and extremely loud barking all day everyday. I reached out to the animal shelter yet again. However, this time for a different animal. It was the same situation as with the rooster; they said unless I found out the specific address of the unit the dog belongs to, there is no course of action the municipality can take.

I even quit resisting my minimalist principals to avoid material objects and purchased a white noise machine on Amazon for about fifty dollars. This electronic device about the size of a softball plugged into an outlet and provided a constant soft fuzzy noise. For the first time in my life I also began using ear plugs on a nightly basis while sleeping.

I sent a second letter to the shelter and explained this canine was likely driven mad from such cruel conditions, and thus it would bark incessantly and wake me up at all hours of the night. Same response as before. No action because the unit number of the dog owner was not known.

In addition to the crazy canine and rowdy rooster, an emergency vehicle with its sirens on passed by about once an hour. Further, a helicopter flew overhead about once an hour as well. Fortunately, those noises were muffled by the white noise machine being on whenever I was home and earplugs whenever I was sleeping. The portable air conditioning unit was even louder than the white noise machine, so during the summers most outside noises were hardly audible.

Eventually I accepted my living situation. I was living here short term to pay off college debt - a sacrifice for easier living and lower stress down the road.

However, this apartment in DTLA where I resided for two years were the worst conditions I ever lived in in America - primarily because of the neighborhood. It was unsafe to walk around at night. The entire neighborhood was graffitied with gang names. There were shady characters walking around during the late hours. The streets smelled of urine and were covered in trash. Up until this point, I have lived in places where I could take an evening stroll around the neighborhood to gather my thoughts and relax. This was the first time in my life I could not enjoy this simple pleasure. At times, the inability to take a meditative walk in the evening made me feel like that German shepherd next door. However, a proper diet of plentiful fruits and vegetables, low sugar, zero caffeine, hardly any processed food, and daily swims or yoga kept me calm so I could overcome the inconvenience of not being able to take a leisurely stroll around the neighborhood after dinner.

Perhaps because these living conditions were extremely irritating, I knew I would not last here long. So I planned to explore as much of Los Angeles as possible.

Chapter 12: Straight Out Of Compton

Since I try to eat relatively healthy and generally avoid cooking meat at home, I tend to eat meat only about once or twice a week - usually on the weekend. One of my favorite guilty pleasures for my weekend meat consumption is barbeque. Now that I was living in LA, I searched "best BBQ in LA" and a restaurant called Bludso's BBQ came up. This dining establishment was in Compton - a city historically associated with gangster rap and gang violence.

The BBQ joint was next door to an establishment called Muhammad Mosque #54 Compton, which had Nation of Islam stickers on the windows. Since this neighborhood was cast in a less than pleasant light in the media, I was a bit apprehensive about dining here. However, as I was in line to order food, four LA County Sheriff's officers got in line behind me. This made me feel a bit more at ease.

I asked the woman taking orders which is better, the pork ribs or brisket. She advised that the lunch special comes with both as well as some sides. I got the two meats with mac n cheese, collard greens, and a piece of cornbread. The meal was massive and only cost about ten dollars. I enjoyed the cuisine in the back where some picnic benches were set up. A damn delicious feast it was.

I drove straight out of Compton. Then I recalled that I heard about a historical monument called Watts Towers. Driving towards this area required that I travel through some neighborhoods that appeared unsavory. The road where this beautiful art display was located was on a dead end street. I drove down, took a look, then drove away. Perhaps the negative media portrayals of this neighborhood kept me from getting out of the car to bask in the enjoyment of this collection of artistic sculptures - some nearly one hundred feet high. I simply observed from my vehicle as I parked next to the structures. The beautiful towers reminded me of art I saw around Barcelona.

Now it was time to find bean pie. I recently learned about bean pie and wanted to experience this culinary creation. Apparently it is a food associated with the Nation of Islam. From my understanding, members of the Nation suggested that eating healthier and avoiding rich foods would help the people associated with this political and religious movement to reduce their chances of obesity and illness compared to their counterparts who would consume fatty and junk foods.

I drove over to Inglewood, California - another area of Los Angeles that has been historically associated with gangs.I found Shabazz Bakery and ordered a slice of bean pie for a couple dollars. It tasted similar to sweet potato pie with a dash of cinnamon. It was nice to have a reason to visit Inglewood to explore this dish of Nation of Islam cuisine.

Chapter 13: Embracing Teetotalism To Pay Off Student Loan Debt - An Analysis Of The Direct And Indirect Costs Of Alcohol

During July 2015 I was a young professional in my late twenties, single, and lived in a large marketplace for dating. One night I found myself at a nearby hipster bar with indie music. I made the acquaintance of a stranger. We spend some time together that evening. A few days later we met for dinner. Later on we shared a bottle of wine at my apartment.

After that weekend, I reflected on the encounters with the woman from the hipster bar. I thought about my plan to pay off my student loan as well as my pursuit of minimalism. Examining my life, I noted that during high school, college, and all of my twenties almost every weekend consisted of going out to a party or bar and having drinks with friends. After I started my career, a friend and I would go out to the bars every weekend. Even though I rarely made it a habit to buy a drink for a woman in exchange for an introduction or an opportunity to mingle, such purchases did happen from time to time. I started to consider the math behind this aspect of courting.

Let's say throughout the course of a Friday evening you purchase five drinks at $10 a piece after tax and tip. In addition, sometimes we would purchase happy hour snacks at about fifteen dollars after tax and tip. Then add post night-out tipsy munchies, such as a late night burrito, which cost another ten dollars. Then cab fare. It is safe to say that a male yuppie with a stable work and living situation in Southern California can spend about one hundred dollars in an evening to partake in "nightlife."

There are also indirect costs associated with a night out on the town on a Friday. On Saturday I would feel a bit groggy and crave junk food. This meant getting BBQ pork ribs or brisket covered in sauce largely composed of sweet syrup and salt. Typically I would also part ways with discipline and feast on some ice cream. Due to the less than healthy way I felt after a night out, I ate more quantity than necessary to satisfy a weekly meat and dessert craving. Not only was this consumption of surplus unhealthy food an additional expense, but it actually made me feel worse the following day. So on Sunday I would crave food to try to restore my health back to normal, such as some vegetable beverage at the juice bar, as well as some coconut water, and a bottle of kombucha. If the original night out cost about one hundred dollars, then adding the junk on Saturday and the "health foods" on Sunday, would bring the total to about one hundred and fifty dollars.

One hundred and fifty dollars each weekend equates to about six hundred bucks a month. Thinking about losing nearly $7,000 a year in order to go out four times a month seemed pretty mind-boggling, especially since I was simply earning a middle class salary.

As I grew older I visited bars less often. But even if you go on a date and you and your date get one glass of wine at one place, that is fifteen dollars each; so thirty bucks total. Then you may want to go to another establishment and have a second glass of wine each. Now you're at sixty dollars. You might want a dessert and perhaps someone even needs some cab fare at some point. One hundred dollars for a simple date, which does not even include a dinner and a movie.

Also, I was approaching thirty years old. I partied away most of my teenage years and most of my twenties. It would be impossible to continue this lifestyle if I wanted to get serious about my finances and my health. Furthermore, I needed to start exploring LA and the surrounding area and learning to love my adopted country of America.

I stopped drinking until my student debt was paid off. Abstinence began July 2015 and lasted nearly a year.

Mentally, I did not think of quitting alcohol as giving up something important and, thereby feeling stress over the loss of a tasty treat. I firmly believed that by ditching drink I actually gained more independence, especially of the financial sort.

More freedom was achieved when I got rid of the alcohol - especially freedom from ill feelings in the morning. I was free to be energized and ready each weekend to begin exploring LA and America.

Chapter 14: Dating On A Budget And Online Dating Versus A More Personable Approach

When I first committed to cutting alcohol and nightlife from my budget back in July 2015 I was worried that it would become difficult to date women. It seemed normal for people to go out for a drink or two to break the ice on a first date. I never abstained from alcohol before. Nor did I ever date someone who did not drink. However, because I was determined to become debt-free I resolved to stick to the following guidelines. A first date would consist of getting a non-alcoholic beverage at a cafe. If there was a second date, I would steer it towards another meetup at a cafe and perhaps this time maybe even get dessert. Depending on chemistry I would propose that a third date would consist of a homemade dinner at my place. If a woman found it forward to have a meal at my place as a third date, I would allow myself to go on one dinner date to a restaurant if prior cafe meetups went particularly well. The restaurant would need to be inexpensive yet interesting, such as an ethnic place where the cost per person was within twenty dollars. By prioritizing my financial goals I made it my mission to avoid paying for endless meals and entertainment as part of courting. If things were going well with the prospective partner, I would need to admit after a few dates that my expectations are for each party to contribute half when going out. After all, I advocate gender equality. If a woman could not understand my goals, there was little business for us being together.

I wondered how I would meet women when avoiding alcohol and nightlife. After committing to this new lifestyle, I tried to meet people at the gym. I was a member of the YMCA in downtown, which offered the best pool in DTLA. Swimming was my primary form of exercise. Only occasionally did I try yoga or lifting weights. Unfortunately, not many women my age swim regularly, at least not at the YMCA.

After a few weeks on the low budget, no alcohol lifestyle I became friendly with a young woman at the gym. We appeared to have some chemistry. Then one day I learned she was very religious. I grew apprehensive. Any connection I thought we had seemed doomed. I am not against any religion but I was agnostic. We hung out a bit. Eventually she told me we could not be together because I was not Christian. That was the first time I was the recipient of such an assertion.

Since I was living frugally I was not meeting many people. LA was a new home for me so I hardly knew anyone. I tried online dating. During this time, smartphone apps such as Tinder were popular for this purpose. Such apps were location based and would show you people who were nearby. Then you swipe your screen one way if you liked their picture and swipe another way if not. The person on the other end would do the same. There was a match when two people liked each others profiles; at which point you were allowed to message each other.

I was not really a fan of this type of dating since I assumed my looks were only average and the primary value I could offer a potential date was my personality. Conveying character is difficult when you are judged by a picture.

During August 2015 I met a young professional online. We decided to meet. She asked a quintessential LA question. When talking about where we lived she inquired as to the name of my building. I thought about how my building is in one of the poorest areas around downtown and does not have a name; only fancy residential buildings have names. Her question struck me as superficial and materialistic, especially since I was living the life of a hermit. Eventually she wanted to go home. I joined her. She wanted to take an Uber ride share despite living a few blocks away. I did not desire life in a fancy building or to pay for a ride to travel a few blocks. I never saw her again.

I met another online date person during August 2015 at a Mexican inspired coffee shop per her request. Horchata latte was offered at this establishment. I never saw cinnamon rice milk as a base for a coffee / decaf beverage before so I was excited to try it. All the seats in the cafe were taken so we walked around downtown with our drinks. I noticed a nice little park of which there are very few in downtown. This park was next to the Fashion Institute of Design and Merchandising. We sat down on a bench in the park. The park was nice and clean. It had trees and a gate around it unlike most parks in DTLA. A homeless woman walked up to us, continued past us, then stopped right behind me behind the bench. She was about two feet from my body. I turned around. She pulled down her pants and started urinating. I was tired so I remained seated as she finished her business. After this point, the conversation between my date and I ceased flowing smoothly.

As I continued to try online dating, many women did not take the time to follow up in person. Of course, it is possible that my aesthetic value in the online dating marketplace was low.

I met another woman from the online dating world, but we did not actually start hanging out till around October 2015. We dated a bit, but there appeared to be a lack of long term compatibility. In all likelihood it seemed that she was neither my type nor was I her type.

Another drawback of online dating is often times there is a lot of messaging before a woman is willing to go on a date in person. Then when you finally meet the person face-to-face, you realize there is absolutely zero chemistry. Alternatively, some of the people you meet look completely different than their photos. For this reason, it is more likely that a person develops arthritis in their smartphone typing finger(s), carpal tunnel syndrome, or neck issues from excessive unnatural bending down to look at their smartphone than finding the love of their life online.

I resolved to try a different approach. Instead of relying on technological advancements, with their promises of making life more efficient and elevating living standards, I went back to the traditional approach employed by individuals around the world before current technology. When I was at a grocery store and there was a woman next to me I might say hi and see if she responds favorably. If so, I may initiate small talk. On rare occasions, this could lead to a phone number, which could possibly result in a date. There were plenty of places where one may find themselves next to a lady - whether it be at a cafe or even at the traffic light waiting to walk across the street. In the two years I walked around DTLA to work, gym, groceries, and errands, I almost never saw the same stranger twice - unless it was someone that worked at a downtown business that I would visit, such as a cashier at Whole Foods with funky hair and tattoos. Those skyscrapers all around have a lot of space for tens of thousands of people inside.

It was important to be cordial and completely avoid any sort of advance that may be deemed unwelcome or any demeanor that could be perceived as having even the slightest hint of aggressiveness. Striking up small talk and conversation with strangers came naturally to me because I lived on the road for two years during the time I held a travel job from 2012 to

2014. Then I traveled around the globe for several months and met new people often. So I was already accustomed to having countless brief conversations with strangers. And I actually enjoyed chatting with random people because I possess an inquisitive mind and firmly believe that there is a lesson to be learned from everyone. Initiating and maintaining dialogue felt relatively simple because I was well traveled, loved to learn about different cultures, perceived my educational background to be a well-rounded one, and had an affinity for arts and history.

Kindly greeting a nearby stranger and engaging in small talk allowed me to display my personality. It is possible some people perceived my demeanor as one characterized by confidence or charisma. Conversely, it is also possible that my chatty disposition came off strange.

Prefering to maintain a sense of independence and self-reliance, I attempted to avoid becoming overly dependent on technology to meet a woman. Since this route of meeting members of the opposite sex in person and outside of bars or restaurants did not appear common I tried my best to be especially perceptive to body cues that might have suggested my approach was off-putting, in which case I could quickly exit. However, it is worth noting that when I gave a greeting I had zero agenda other than to give a greeting. When I engaged in small talk I wanted nothing other than to engage in small talk. And if there was a date, I wanted nothing other than to enjoy the date and get to know a new person.

Ultimately, I discovered that some women were receptive to this straightforward and light-hearted approach because it took courage. Hardly many men were able to strike up conversation with a passing stranger in such a friendly and not overly eager or disrespectful manner. Therefore, some women appeared to be appreciative of my affable approach. It definitely was not ostentatious display of wealth that captivated any audience.

Chapter 15: Will She Judge Me For My Tiny Apartment? Embracing My Values To Attract Potential Partners With Similar Beliefs

Now that I was becoming more comfortable meeting women in the large potential dating pool that is DTLA, I began to reflect on my hang ups. I needed to get over thinking that I was less than an ideal partner because I was living in a tiny apartment in a poor neighborhood, abstaining from drink and nightlife, and rarely partaking in restaurants and lavish entertainment. As a young child growing up in San Diego, I attended a typical public high school where you were judged by your shoes and clothes. It seemed that teenage guys who came from wealthier families dated prettier girls. While I did my best to fit in with my group of American-born friends, I felt that my immigrant background and poor parents made me an outlier. Perhaps this insecurity was unfounded. It is possible that my eccentric personality made me more of an oddball in the eyes of females than Slavic ethnicity or socioeconomic status. Nonetheless, when you grow up listening to rap music for most of your teenage years, you cannot help but feel the influence of materialism in the mate selection process.

Eventually I tried to accept myself as I was. I convinced myself that a reasonably understanding woman would be sympathetic to my LA goals. Such a woman would see my living situation as one that reflects discipline, ability to delay gratification, and power to resist temptation. Thus, I convinced myself that the aspects of my life which initially caused self-doubt were actually positive attributes. After all, it is hardly simple for many in America to save half of their after tax income. Many Americans are living paycheck to paycheck and without a rainy day fund.

Changing my perspective empowered me to move forward with a minimalist lifestyle. Acceptance of my values allowed me to feel less self-conscious about my situation when speaking with potential partners. I was glad to finally overcome outdated notions that most women desire a rich man. As society was moving toward more gender equality, women were able to embark on successful careers. According to some, characteristics such as personality, values, and how a man treated people mattered more than how well a male could provide.

Chapter 16: The Date Who Criticised My Minimalist Life For Hours And Drove Me To Leave The Online Dating World, Judging A Woman's iPhone Watch, And Finding Someone Who Accepted My Values

Around August 2015 I found out that a woman I spent time with in New York City a couple years before, moved to LA. Our time together in Manhattan seemed pleasant so I thought we could rekindle a friendship. We met in September 2015 and went to Venice Beach with some of her friends. It was a relaxing day at the sea; until I saw a police helicopter flying low near the sand to patrol the beachgoers. I grew up going to the beach in San Diego most of my childhood. We did not have such bizarre security measures. LA is too crowded. At one point during my LA years, a colleague informed me that in Los

Angeles, most of the dead are buried standing up because of the cost of subterranean real estate in cemeteries.

The woman from NYC and her friends were drinking that day I met her. When we arrived back at her place someone ordered a six pack of Corona via a mobile app. This was the first time I heard of alcohol delivery. These individuals I was hanging out with were getting ready to go out on the town in West Hollywood to party at the gay bars. By this point I was already tired of being around alcohol the entire day. I decided to head home shortly after we arrived at the club. I needed to stay away from party people to avoid spending on Uber car rides and over-priced, unhealthy restaurants. Furthermore, herding tipsy folk was not enjoyable. Simply hanging out with people who are drinking can add up in costs even if you are not consuming alcohol.

Despite my failure at trying to court a woman who I dated previously, I quit using online dating sites around September 2015. Even though my first dates that came from approaching a woman in public rather than online were hardly promising, they were better than the date which led me to finally delete the Tinder app from my phone.

This date occurred September 2015. After electronic communication for a couple weeks we finally met at a coffee shop around 4 p.m. I prefer to keep first dates to about an hour unless it goes super well. Initial dates are a good way to weed out lack of chemistry without too much time commitment. If there is chemistry it will usually flow better on the second date after the awkwardness of meeting a stranger is gone. She told me she wanted to avoid traffic so she would not begin driving home till 7 p.m. Then I felt forced into a three hour meet and greet. Even if you do not have a car, LA traffic still affects your life.

The discussion became more of an interview. She was older and wanted marriage quickly, so she needed to conduct her due diligence rather than let the conversation flow at its own pace. She started by telling me how strange it was that I do not own a car, and that it must be weird to be in a small geographical bubble most of the time. I told her I liked walking places and there were ways to get around if I needed to. I mentioned that I once heard someone say "LA has so many people, but everyone is so lonely" and that I interpreted the statement to be a result of most people having to sit by themselves in a car for two hours a day. She continued to express unease at my choice to live without personal car ownership. I suggested that most of America associated LA with two characteristics - pollution and traffic - and both of these are brought on by excess personal vehicles. The intent of my lifestyle choice was to help in what little way I could to limit these worst aspects of LA. She said one person's actions did not matter. I wanted to ask her if she ever heard of voting.

That I would fit in well in Santa Monica because it is a healthy community full of yogis was her next comment to me after I mentioned my interest in health and life experiences over career and home ownership. As I walked the woman to her car she mentioned I am thin and that she is used to dating bigger guys. Throughout the date she made me feel inadequate - like no other first date has made me feel. Perhaps it was a bad day at the office for her. So I texted her a couple weeks later. She advised that I was not what she was looking for. I am grateful for the horrible three hour interview complete with judgments since that was the small cost I paid for the motivation to start a new chapter in life - one without technology for a fundamental human desire - companionship. Besides, initially meeting a stranger in public rather than online allows you to pick up on how they feel about you from their body language before even going on a first date.

Around this time I met a young professional woman while walking to the gym. I usually preferred to go to a cafe for a first date to keep my expenses low but she insisted we go for a drink. My abstinence from booze saved me a few bucks. We had a pleasant evening and, physically, she was my type. Unfortunately, I quickly learned that she only recently exited a long term relationship. Because I thought the chemistry was so good and her beauty so appealing, I felt let down. Thus, I resolved to learn from this situation. Information on the net seemed to suggest a good rule of thumb for dating people who have recently left a significant other is: time of last relationship multiplied by half. In other words, if you go on a date with a woman and you find out she was in a three year relationship that ended two months ago, it is safe to assume she is likely not ready to move on to someone else. So from that point on when I would go on a date with a new person, I would try to respectfully get a bit more information on when the last relationship ended and how much time passed. If it was a year long relationship and six months passed, then great. In such instance, the probability of finding a significant other in this person would be better.

During November 2015 I met a woman at a traffic signal while we were waiting to cross the street. We only dated briefly as she was leaving the country soon. This encounter reinforced my belief that it was better to meet a stranger to date at an intersection than to find someone online.

Around December 2015 I was consuming some nutrition in the dining area of the newly opened Whole Foods in DTLA. There was a woman sitting next to me. We began to chat. Eventually we dated for a bit. It was true, you did not need the internet to date women.

I met another woman while seeking food at Grand Central Market in DTLA. We ended up going on a date to a cafe. Then we met again. Eventually I offered to prepare dinner for her. She came over and we hung out. I began to realize that my guideline for budget dating is actually possible. It helped that I was learning how to cook more interesting dishes.

While maintaining relations with the woman I met at Whole Foods and the woman from Grand Central Market, I met another woman at the gym. She was an athletic young professional.

The woman from the gym and I met at a cafe during December 2015. She had plans after our date so I felt she was a bit rushed. It was not an ideal situation from my perspective but I understood since it was a major holiday. Conversation went well but then I noticed an Apple iPhone watch on her wrist. This was the first woman I attempted to court that wore such a device. Being a minimalist, I found myself having judgemental thoughts. My brain was unable to understand wearing a smartphone on your wrist if you already have one in your pocket. We Americans are becoming overly dependent on and distracted by technology. Technology can be good if we control it but many people allow tech to control them.

She was beautiful, interesting, and athletic. I was a hermit who was opposed to constant beeping from notifications by our technological overlords who never leave our side. Her iPhone watch brought out my insecurities. The gadget reminded me of previously held beliefs that women desire a man who can provide them with luxuries. Of course, this was all in my head. For all I know, she could have afforded dozens of these gizmos with her own earnings. But my neural networks are somewhat flawed like every other human on the planet.

Shortly after, we went on a second date to a hip yet relatively inexpensive restaurant in DTLA that specialized in conical Japanese hand rolls. These rolls were similar to sushi but much less formal and much more approachable. To save money on this date I avoided alcohol. I got the sense that she was a well established young professional who was accustomed to a higher standard of living than the average Angeleno. If my mind were more robust I could have focused more on the positive attributes of this individual, such as her keenness to discuss mindfulness and meditation during our second date. But alas, my brain latched on to the Apple Watch and could not let go. My dive into minimalism allowed me to let go of many material possessions but I was far from mastering letting go of thoughts that could hold back a person just as attachments to possessions can. I was able to resist owning an iPhone watch but I could not resist my own negative thoughts and judgements about such device owned by someone else.

I judged the woman from the gym to be super serious about busy business and capitalistic concerns. At this point in my life I was not much of a career man and modes of deriving joy from the world did not involve climbing the corporate ladder. Nonetheless, I attempted to continue to maintain some relations with her even though I had the impression that I was not at the top of her list of potential suitors. Ironically, it was hypocritical of me to assume she was always busy and multitasking. Even though I was not preoccupied with tasks to advance my career prospects, I was attempting to juggle various prospective relationships.

While trying to maintain conversations with these three women I met another woman near the gym. Shortly after, I saw her again and asked if she wanted to meet for coffee. I found a cozy cafe in Little Tokyo and we had an enjoyable evening. Second date was at a relatively inexpensive restaurant in Little

Tokyo. No, she was not Japanese; I simply enjoyed Little Tokyo because back in those days it seemed like the only part of DTLA that was relatively clean and safe. For the third date I invited her to a yoga class at the gym where we were both members. A budget friendly date.

After a few dates, she seemed elegant, cultured, and from a well-to-do upbringing. Thus, I avoided telling her that I lived car-free. I was still insecure about how LA residents, with their automobile obsession, would feel about my iconoclastic ways. Most of the Angelenos I told up to this point expressed shock at my car-free life.

Around December 2015 I found myself courting four women simultaneously. All four worked in DTLA and within a one mile radius of each other. Two of them worked around the corner from one another. Two of them went to the same gym. Since I walked everywhere and occasionally walked with one of these women, I hoped another would not spot me. Because there are thousands of souls wandering around downtown everyday, I never ran into a woman I was attempting to charm while walking with another lady.

Dating one person is difficult. Trying to court four individuals was exhausting. There were times when I had a date with four different women planned for four consecutive days, which is challenging when one has a full time job. The conversations began to blur and it became increasingly hard to remember which detail applied to which woman.

Shortly after meeting the fourth woman I realized that I felt comfortable with her. She was kind, caring, intelligent, and independent. Best of all, she understood me, my values, and my goals. We became official during January 2016. As our relationship grew, I learned a lot about her, myself, Los Angeles, and America.

Chapter 17: The Diversity Of LA's Dating Pool And Learning How To Be Comfortable In My Own Skin To Know What To Look For In A Suitable Partner

Within my first seven months of living downtown, I went on dates with women from the following backgrounds: Anglo, Armenian, Filipina, Indian, Mexican, Salvadoran, Thai, and Vietnamese. LA truly was a melting pot. Dating such women allowed me to learn about myself as much as I learned about them.

The world traveling nomad in me was excited to spend time with a female from far away lands who introduced me to her cuisine as we dined at an inexpensive restaurant in an ethnic enclave in LA. It was cool to have an experience similar to international travel while being only a few miles from my apartment in America. During my late twenties I always hoped for these types of experiences while roaming around various countries abroad. Such adventures can be thrilling when first experienced due to their novelty. However, the more I dated this woman the more I learned about myself. I was an American, and for long term compatibility I need someone with an excellent command of English. Looks and money are not features I have very much. So I like to think that the only feature I can offer is my personality, which is easy-going, open-minded, adventurous, and being a fan of lifelong learning; but more importantly by traits such as being silly. Comedy was perhaps my greatest coping mechanism when dealing with stress. I tend to make lame observations, dad jokes, horrible puns, word play, and a host of other comments. Regardless of whether my observation, comment, or joke is not funny to the woman I am dating, it is comforting to me if she understands what I am trying to get at - even if she rolls her eyes. If a potential partner was unable to understand some obscure cultural reference in relation to a horrible pun, then I saw little point of being with such a woman.

Furthermore, I desired to be a giving partner who was helping create a mutually beneficial and meaningful experience for both individuals. Long periods of deep conversation are required before each party is comfortable opening up about their desires. These two aspects of long term dating are increasingly complex when someone lacks an advanced level of your language. And I was unwilling to learn the language of some distant land.

While dating professional business women in the big opportunistic land of capitalism, I also discovered that I should not have been self conscious about my minimalist lifestyle. Some women in this megapolis were worried a man would only be with them because of their wealth. This type of woman appreciates someone who is humble, and is able to resist the temptation of desiring more than he can afford. Insights such as these served as a reminder that there are women who care more about personality and values than the material possessions and type of shelter a mate can provide. Such women do not care to be wowed by the location of the date. They understand that a date or two at a cafe, then a budget friendly meal together is enough to weed out characters one is not keen to pursue further. I got the impression that what mattered most was confidence, time, and persistence. Confidence was gained by being true to yourself and pursuing your own personal goals - such as health, financial, intellectual, and adventure-oriented. Time was necessary for successful dating because the modern woman is a busy individual. There are times she may need to cancel a date, shows up late, or is simply having a bad day. To attain success in most endeavors, you need persistence in order to deal with failure and to pick yourself up and try again. Dating requires a lot of failure - whether being stood up or spending a lot of time meeting people with whom relations do not work out.

During my first few months in LA, I learned that this area of the country is about 50% Hispanic. I read that Los Angeles has the third highest population of Mexicans of any city in the world after Mexico City and Guadalajara. Apparently LA has the largest number of Mexicans of any city outside of Mexico. While most of the Hispanics in LA are of Mexican descent, there are many Latinos from El Salvador, Guatemala, and various other Latin American countries. I learned it is important to be mindful when using various terms to describe people.

It was interesting to date Mexican women with roots from various regions such as Jalisco, Oaxaca, and Yucatan. Upon learning about the diversity of Mexico I wanted to experience the variety of Mexican regional cuisine offered in LA.

Chapter 18: Eating Grasshoppers, One Of The Best Foods I Ate In LA Over Two Years Cost Only A Few Dollars, And LA As A Microcosm - A Budget-Friendly World Food Tour Of The City's Ethnic Enclaves

With DTLA undergoing rapid gentrification, the Grand Central Market was becoming a hip place with a variety of ethnic dishes rather than folks selling produce among greasy food stands. The people watching was enjoyable, and the food was delicious yet inexpensive. However, you have to deal with eating in a market rather than at a sit down restaurant. Loud environment and long lines, but a fun place nonetheless.

One particular place in the market that I enjoyed was an old school legacy establishment selling mole sauce - a traditional Mexican cuisine. Mole sauces can be made out of various combinations of fruits, peppers, spices, nuts, seeds, chocolate, etc. There are many variations based on the region of Mexico and the family recipe. This stall offered about a dozen different mole sauces in various colors such as light green, reddish brown, brown, and black like tar. The vendor let me sample all for free. I would purchase some, cook with water in a pan, and pour over a dish of cooked grain and sauteed vegetables.

Another establishment inside the Grand Central Market was a Thai food restaurant. The kanom krok Thai coconut rice pudding pancakes were served hot, tasted delicious, and were cheap. There are many Thai restaurants around LA and the country but it is rare for most to offer this dessert.

Grand Central Market also housed a Salvadoran food establishment that specialized in pupusas, which is perhaps the most common foods associated with El Salvador. A pupusa is a thick tortilla usually stuffed with cheese but also other types of filling. Typically it is served with a fermented cabbage slaw called curtido, which is like a Latin version of sauerkraut. During conversations with a Salvadoran woman I was courting, she mentioned she ate at all the Salvadoran restaurants in LA and that the pupusas served at the place in Grand Central Market taste the most like those in her home country. LA has a large Salvadoran community and pupusas can be found throughout the city. They are an inexpensive cultural experience.

Since I spent two years living in Austin, Texas and loved BBQ, I was extremely pleased that there was a Texas style smoked BBQ establishment called Horse Thief at Grand Central Market. The smoked brisket reminded me of my time in Austin and it was the perfect way to indulge in my weekend treat of red meat - especially after a morning swim a few blocks away.

In a post 2010 world, as the majority of the US population began owning a smartphone, social media became increasingly popular and more instantaneous. Along with this technological evolution, taking pictures of food and posting them to social media became one of the nation's favorite pastimes. Food not only needed to taste good, but it also needed to be photogenic. One place in Grand Central Market that was cherished by the yuppies and hipsters was called Eggslut. This establishment always had the longest line of any business in Grand Central Market. They specialized in various sandwiches with an egg. Eventually, I felt obliged to see what the hype was about. The "Gaucho" came with seared tri-tip steak, chimichurri, and an egg on a brioche bun. It was delicious; and as beautiful as all the people in line.

After arriving in LA, I quickly learned that one of the best places for authentic tacos was a chain called King Taco. They offered al pastor, which was cooked on a device that spins the meat while heating it. I saw the same style of cooking during my teenage visits to Tijuana. This is a must for any LA visitor. Los Angeles has more Mexicans and Mexican-Americans than San Diego, so they have better Mexican food despite being further away from the border. Another taco place locals told me about was Guisados. They specialized in handmade tortillas that were more puffy than typical ones. This local business offered much more variety of braises than most other taco spots.

Tacos are such a staple of LA food culture that a new fusion cuisine became wildly popular - Korean tacos sold from food trucks. As the name suggests, Korean marinated meat was served in a taco tortilla and topped with kimchi as well as guacamole and salsa. The food truck was an important aspect of LA food culture - and Korean tacos were one of the shining stars.

Even though I grew up about twenty miles from Mexico, my knowledge of that country's cuisine was limited. Now that I was in LA, there was a lot of catching up on this front. Fortunately, Olvera Street - a historic Spanish district - was located a couple miles from my apartment. Situated between Chinatown and Little Tokyo, this tourist area offers plenty of Mexican restaurants, shops, and monuments. I needed to try a Mexican dish I heard about for a long time - pozole. Other than meats, veggies, and spices, the distinguishing ingredient in this traditional Mexican soup is hominy. The hot soup is ideal on a winter day. While in this quaint strip of dining establishments and retailers, I also tried the stuffed churros at Mr Churro. These Mexican pastries made of fried dough and covered in sugar and cinnamon are even better at this food purveyor because they are filled with various sweet sauces. A couple of my favorites include the churro stuffed with caramel as well as those filled with custard.

As I was meeting people in LA and researching the cuisine of various Hispanic cultures, I learned about champurrado. This winter warmer from Mexico is essentially a hot chocolate drink thickened with corn dough. Different recipes call for the addition of various spices.

Since the Philippines was a colony of Spain for hundreds of years, Filipino culture acquired some similar foods as Spain and other countries under its rule. The Filipino version of champurrado is called champorado and is similar except that instead of corn dough as the thickening agent, this version of this dessert from the Philippines is essentially a hot chocolate rice porridge. Since I loved chocolate I was pleased that my explorations of LA's Historic Filipinotown led me to find this tasty sweet treat.

My hometown of San Diego has a large Filipino presence. From my understanding, this was a result of San Diego's historic role as a military post. I was told many people from the Philippines came to this Southern California city after World War II. As I was growing up my mom was friends with many Filipinos. One of my most memorable desserts from childhood was turon. Turon is a fried spring roll with banana inside which is fried and caramelized with sweet goodness on the outside. Living in proximity to Historic Filipinotown allowed me to indulge in this sweet snack from the Philippines. I took a date to get turon and she loved her first experience with them. Trying all these novel and delicious foods is a great way to date on a budget and see areas of the city not often frequented by many Angelenos or tourists.

Another notable Filipino culinary experience I enjoyed while living in LA was dinner at LA Rose Cafe, which was established in 1982. I was told about a traditional Filipino red meat stew made with peanut butter. Since I love peanut butter I felt a yearning to try it. I ordered the Kare Kare - beef oxtail and cheek stewed in peanut sauce with eggplant, bok choy, and green beans. While it did not appear that the peanut sauce was actually peanut butter, the meal was fantastic. I also got some halayang for dessert. This sweet treat is purple yam, which is grated, then cooked with coconut milk till it is thickened. LA Rose Cafe is super cozy and is decorated as if it were someone's living room. I dined on a wicker chair with a pillow near my lower back while a guy played piano.

Getting back to the cuisine of Mexico, my love of mole sauce led me to an eatery that specializes in this subtly chocolatey condiment. The restaurant called Guelaguetza was established in 1994 and is also an advocate for Oaxacan culture in the LA area. Eating here was the first time I tried the Mexican delicacy of fried grasshoppers called chapulines. A few dozen of the bugs were served in a bowl made out of tortilla. The grasshoppers can be added on top of other food to add an earthy flavor and crunch. A novel experience and not horrible as some might imagine. Even if one has zero interest in fried bugs, the mole sauce and tamales wrapped in banana leaves here are great. The restaurant has an authentic atmosphere and includes a stage for live music and a little retail market in the corner selling sweets and boutique goods.

Another regional Mexican restaurant is Chichen Itza near the University of Southern California. This dining establishment specializes in Yucatan style dishes. The cochinita pibil is an authentic Yucatan dish. Chaya is a Mayan leafy green that is made into a juice and is also available at this restaurant. The drink is refreshing and low in sugar content. Even the tacos are amazing - the meat was lightly crispy with a slight resemblance to fried pork rings (ie, skin) except not as fatty. This was one of the best tacos I ate in LA.

The Mexican food scene in LA was so robust that we even savored ice cream sandwiches where the two outside cookie parts of the sandwich were flattened discs of churro, covered with cinnamon and sugar. I loved churros and I loved ice cream. So logically I also loved ice cream between two churros.

Since I lived near a Guatemalan community, I needed to try their cuisine. Conveniently, there was a small Guatemalan restaurant in a strip mall one block from my apartment. In addition to my love for fried banana spring rolls that are caramelized (turon), I also have a weakness for fried plantains. So I was excited when I first learned of this mouthwatering dessert offered at this restaurant. Plantains stuffed with black beans, chocolate, and cinnamon are pressed into a ball shape then fried. This is called rellenitos and it is a food I have not heard anyone mention in my life, but are a must try.

Another helpful tip I learned from exploring Guatemalan food is that tamales from this country are different than those from Mexico. As a general guideline, most Mexican tamales served in LA are prepared in corn husks. However, Guatemalan tamales are wrapped in banana leaves. Both need to be experienced. Also, around the holidays, Guatemalan tamales can be made with prunes, raisins, and olive, which makes them more delicious.

Since I lived in a predominantly Hispanic area, I also shopped at chain grocery stores that made sure to cater to the tastes of the local patrons. So I had the joy of being able to purchase two types of non-traditional fruits from these super markets. This was the first time I ate fresh prickly pear and guava.

Los Angeles has a significant Jewish community, which has a large presence around Fairfax Avenue just south of West Hollywood. I found an iconic Jewish deli near downtown called Langer's. Apparently this Jewish deli has been in business for a long time. The pastrami on rye is phenomenal.

Near Fairfax is a shopping complex called The Grove. While wandering around this neighborhood I found a Malaysian inspired restaurant that offered kaya toast. Kaya is a coconut jam with the color and consistency of custard. It is served between two slices of bread like a grilled cheese sandwich but sweet. Up until eating this delicious dessert in

LA, I only ate it once - in Singapore. I was shocked that LA now offered such rare ethnic foods. I took a date here so she could try this delight that she never heard about. She loved kaya.

When committing to live on a low budget in order to pursue financial goals, you generally want to avoid taking a date out for sushi. For some reason, many sushi places end up being expensive. Since I was living in Southern California, the weather rarely got me craving for soup, so I was hardly a fan of ramen restaurants. But I do love meat skewers. Eastern Europeans love to barbeque meat on skewers. Japanese cuisine has restaurants that focus on meat skewers called yakitori. These types of Japanese restaurants are relatively rare (at least compared to sushi and ramen) and, therefore, I found them to be a cool type of food to introduce to a date. As an added benefit, yakitori spots are generally fairly budget-friendly. The meat skewers include various types of chicken such as chicken meatball and chicken breast to other less common parts of the chicken such as heart and gizzard. Beef tongue skewers are one of my favorites. There are also vegetarian options such as mushrooms on a little wooden skewer stick. The Little Tokyo neighborhood offered a great restaurant that served these yakitori and that was light on the wallet.

Little Tokyo was also home to a mochi ice cream establishment. Mochi is a glutinous rice that can be made into a ball shaped dessert stuffed with ice cream. These frozen treats have been becoming exceedingly popular and accessible around the US. Nonetheless, this Little Tokyo purveyor of mochi ice cream offered authentic flavors like black sesame as well as red bean.

While providing highlights from this Japanese enclave of DTLA, it is worth mentioning a notable dining establishment that was authentic yet affordable - Marugame Monzo. This restaurant specialized in hand-pulled udon noodle soup. What gave the spot an extra bit of wow-factor was that you can see the kitchen staff working the noodles out in the open. One of the most famous dishes here was the sea urchin cream udon. Another great example of dishes that can be feasted upon in LA as a once a week splurge on the weekend without too much of a dent in the cash flow going to savings.

Thai Town was a cool neighborhood that had a few blocks of Thai restaurants and businesses. Nowadays there are Thai restaurants all over the country - even in small towns. I have been a big fan of Thai dishes since college days where I first discovered Pad Thai. However, there was one Thai food here that I have never seen anywhere before: Thai tea custard. I used to love Thai tea, with its flavor of sweet and spice. And now I found this custard that was that same flavor made into a silky smooth pudding that was heavenly.

In LA I worked with Taiwanese and Chinese people. On occasion, these kind folks would invite me to join them for lunch, allowing me to learn more about Chinese cuisine. Sometimes we would go to San Gabriel Valley (SGV). The town of San Gabriel, California was a central area in SGV and was about ten miles from DTLA. SGV has an extremely large population of Chinese and Taiwanese.

One memorable Chinese dish I tried in SGV was jiuniang - a sweet fermented rice porridge. It was like a typical rice porridge but lightly sweetened and tasted as if there were a few drops of rice liquor inside. This treat warmed the soul.

The most novel food I tried in SGV was Xinjiang Uyghur food. Xinjiang is a region in China. Uyghurs are ethnically Turkish people living in this territory. This type of food is Islamic, which I can appreciate since this cuisine has a lot of lamb. One of the staples of this regional Chinese cuisine is spicy cumin lamb skewers. This dish was phenomenal - one of my favorites from my two years in LA. The establishment called Omar Restaurant was a small mom and pop shop with Muslim art and a thick rug with an image of Mecca on the wall. It seemed more like a Middle Eastern establishment than any other Chinese eatery in which I ever dined.

Other notable eats worth trying in LA's Asian area of SGV is Taiwanese hot pot. The establishment we dined at offered peanut sauce as an option for one of the types of broth. This was delicious. A second must try restaurant is Din Tai Fung, a Taiwanese restaurant specializing in steamed dumplings. Din Tai Fung has locations in major wealthy metropolitan areas around the world.

My Chinese and Taiwanese colleagues and I also dined in Chinatown since it was closer to DTLA. While in the company of these folks, I learned about abalone. I later made a trip back to Chinatown to try this delicacy. It tasted like a fancier and more delicious form of calamari. Luckily, the place I tried abalone at in Chinatown had small ones so I could stay within budget.

Since I loved the spicy cumin lamb skewers in the predominantly Asian and Asian American area of San Gabriel Valley, I wondered if there were any restaurants serving this dish closer to me. I found a restaurant in Koreatown that appeared to be Korean and Chinese. They offered spicy cumin lamb skewers, and interestingly, the menu also listed bull penis meat skewers. I figured I would try this phallus. It was a cook your own meat on the grill place, but the staff helped me figure out when meat items were cooked to perfection. The texture of the penis was like tendon and was not particularly appetizing.

There were places in K-town that served up some mouth-watering meals. One such establishment was called Yellow House Cafe, which is more of a fusion restaurant than traditional Korean. The business is in a converted house with a lovely dining area in the backyard, which is relatively closed off from the neighborhood, and gives you a brief respite from the negative attributes of big city living. An outstanding signature dish of theirs is the pasta cooked with a cream sauce that is prepared with kimchi and bacon.

Another interesting variety of Asian cuisine that can be found in LA is food from Burma. I tried the national dish of Burma, Mohinga, which is a soup of rice noodles and catfish chowder. Another popular Burmese dish is tea leaf salad. The tea leaves taste like bitter olives but they offer a distinctive culinary experience. Dessert consisted of a trifecta of cakes - semolina wheat cake with poppy seeds; cake of tapioca, coconut milk and white rice flour; and cake of cassava flour and egg. I enjoyed the cuisine so much that I later went to another restaurant featuring this country's food to feast on fish grilled in banana leaf.

During June 2016 I took a vacation to Kauai, Hawaii. While there I first tried pressed sugar cane juice made of a local high quality cane, which gave the drink a dark olive brown color. I fell in love with this refreshment. So I went on a mission to find cane juice when I got back to LA. The one in Chinatown uses a low quality traditional sugar cane, so the juice is not as tasty. Then I found a small business in Little Armenia that specializes in cane juice. Raw Cane Super Juice as the business is called uses a higher end cane plant which makes the juice more delicious. This drink became a post-hike staple on the weekends.

I went to Little Armenia to try their cuisine. I stumbled upon a bakery that served authentic and delicious breads, of which the lahmajoun (also known as Armenian pizza) is delicious. This feast inspired more research of Armenian cuisine and I found more treats at a restaurant called 10e, which was in DTLA. We tried the spicy Armenian sausage called sujuk flambe as well as a trio of traditional savory pastries.

In hopes of trying food that was more authentic to Armenian cuisine I went to Glendale, where the largest concentration of Armenians in the US live. Raffi's Place was recommended by a colleague from Armenia. I was told this restaurant was actually Persian but supposedly offered some Armenian dishes since there was a large Armenian flight into Iran after the Armenian Genocide. Two appetizers I ordered which I never saw at any other restaurants before were tadig ("rice crust") topped with stews called ghormeh sabzi and gheimeh. The second dish, kashk o'bademjan, was caramelized onions and kashk (whey) served on a bed of fried eggplant.

My foray into Armenian cuisine came to an end when I found out about grape sujuk. Sujuk actually means sausage. This candy was not a sausage but looked like one. Basically, walnuts are tied along a thin string, then dipped in grape juice that has been thickened by heat and flour. When this dries, the string can be removed. Then you have something that looks like a sausage, but is actually a dessert. I was glad to have tried all these novel Armenian foods while living in a city where this community thrives.

LA's affordable food scene was more diverse than I expected. I even found an Austrian bakery in DTLA where I was able to reminisce on my travels around Vienna while eating a pork schnitzel served with freshly grated horseradish. I was excited since I first tried freshly grated horseradish root in Vienna and have never seen it on a menu in the States before. Being a big fan of marzipan, I was unable to resist trying the poppyseed and marzipan pastry as well.

There was also Belgian style fries and sausage served at the Belgian ale focused beer hall called Wurstkuche in the gentrifying Arts District. This place has been extremely popular among the hip young Angelenos. Sometimes the line was out the door, but the fries were some of the best in town. However, for a beer centric setting I preferred Firestone Walker Brewing Company's location about a dozen blocks from Venice Beach. Whiskey barrel aged beers and sour ales were on tap at this location of this well renowned Central California brewery. After spending an afternoon walking or cycling along the sea, with tens of thousands of other people, Firestone Walker was an ideal place to escape from crowds because it was far enough away from any major tourist area near the beach. This establishment was a place where one could enjoy an elaborate brew in relative peace after the frustration of bicycle traffic jams on the boardwalk.

Outside of Los Angeles but within LA County, Long Beach is home to a large Cambodian community. Cambodia Town is near central Long Beach and is home to a large concentration of Cambodian restaurants and businesses. This ethnic enclave is only about one hour by subway from DTLA. This area is worth exploring to try cuisine from this Asian country.

Further away from central LA and well into Orange County is a city called Westminster. This town is home to one of the largest Vietnamese communities in the country. Little Saigon is the center of this Vietnamese community. There are dozens of restaurants that serve cuisine from this Asian country. I found joy in being able to take a deeper dive into Vietnamese cuisine beyond pho soup. One of my favorite dishes is a thick crepe-like pancake made out of rice flour which is folded over in half and stuffed with shrimp, pork, and bean sprouts. It is called banh xeo. Since fresh pressed sugarcane juice is a staple of South Asia, this refreshment is available in Little Saigon.

Eating my way around greater LA during 2015 - 2017 felt like I traveled around the world without leaving the comfort of a Western apartment and job. I was amazed by the array of cuisine offered in this small region of the globe. The variety of food reflected the extensive backgrounds in America. As I continued to meet people from various backgrounds and as I dined in restaurants surrounded by people from all over the world, I began to appreciate cultural diversity as one of the benefits of life in my adopted country. Individuals around the globe would sacrifice everything for the opportunity to reside in America because they believed that by living in the US, they could be the person that they were in their heart. Not many countries offer this opportunity. As an immigrant, I often felt a sense of joy to be surrounded by so many other foreign-born folks who, like me, were simply trying to make the best of the opportunities available to them in this country. People who relocated to the US appeared grateful to live without the fear they faced in their home country - whether persecution, violence, corruption, pollution, or even nuclear disaster. I got the feeling that most of us new Americans simply wanted to earn a fair wage, pay our taxes, contribute to our community in some little way that we could, and have our perspectives and opinions incorporated into society in order to create a better and more welcoming nation for all.

Chapter 19: She Drew A Picture Of A Microwave For Me Because I Did Not Own Such A Device - Freeing Myself From Stuff

Despite the grand culinary adventure during two years in LA, I rarely ate at restaurants that cost more than mid range. Often times I would eat at establishments on the lower price range. I cannot recall a time when I paid for a steak at a high end restaurant in the greater Los Angeles area. It is possible that it may have happened once or twice but I found such cuisine and environment too bourgeois. In addition, I was required to wear a tie to work during the week so I did not want to dress up on my days off.

I noticed when consuming energy (e.g., food) and not depleting it efficiently by creating movement (e.g., exercise), my body would become lethargic and ill. Similarly, my soul felt unbalanced when I consumed food prepared by others or consumed experiences without ever creating. I felt a strong urge to create. Thus, I pursued minimalism as a means of creating a strategy to rely less on material possessions.

After college whenever I lived alone I always lived in a studio apartment rather than a one bedroom. The rent was cheaper and since I lacked many possessions I hardly needed much space. I estimate that in cities like San Diego, Austin, and Los Angeles, studios are about $300 less per month than a one bedroom. If you factor in heating and AC costs for an apartment with more square footage, it may be reasonable to assume this could average out to be an additional $50 a month. Thus, I estimate it costs an additional $350 a month for a one bedroom. This amounts to $4,200 a year. Presumably I lived in studios rather than a one bedroom apartment for six years. In total, my willingness to live in a smaller and more cozy space presented me with the opportunity to save approximately $25,000 over the six years. This amount of money is a sizeable amount to put towards a downpayment on a home. Alternatively, twenty five grand could last me a year of travel to mid range price countries or two years around poorer countries.

I was more than happy to live in a studio rather than a one bedroom because I derive joy from efficiency and resourcefulness. In addition, the last time I personally owned a television in my own residence was when I lived in a dorm room in college. I enjoyed watching films, but DVDs could be played on the large screen of my iMac desktop computer set up near my bed. As the internet grew, movies could be streamed on a laptop. When employed full time, I would rarely watch movies or television shows more than a few hours a week. After coming home from work where I would spend the entire day staring at a screen, I much preferred to read, swim, take a long stroll outside, practice yoga, or lift some light weights. I figured expanding my mind with books and adding years to my health as well as health to my years with exercise was more productive than endless consumption of watching films and shows on a screen.

Since I had zero television, there was zero need for a DVD player. Nor did I need to furnish my residence with an entertainment center on which to place such material possessions. Watching a movie or two each week on my laptop from my bed was sufficient. No woman who I dated and with whom I watched a film in bed on a laptop seemed to mind the lack of giant big screen theater complete with fancy entertainment center. Frankly, I am unsure I would date someone who watched the screen an hour a day after work as a habit.

Before I moved to Los Angeles, I lived in Ventura for about a couple months. During this time I used a microwave approximately once per week. I would nuke a potato for seven minutes, mash it with a fork, and dump a can of sardines and olive oil on top. If I ever had left overs from a restaurant or some extra grains in the rice cooker, I much preferred to heat them on the pan since the microwave tended to leave the food super hot in some spots and cold in others. Sometimes I would heat food in the microwave and the bowl would be scorching but the meal inside was still cold. It took longer to heat up food in a pan but it was worth the extra few minutes to have better tasting food. Shortly after moving to LA, I ditched the microwave during late 2015. Instead of heating my weekly potato in this electronic device, I would chop a potato and fry it in a pan. This new method of cooking a potato increased the prep time from seven minutes to half an hour. Despite the additional time required, I actually enjoyed cooking. Cooking became a healthy and creative outlet to relax from stress.

I pondered the philosophical underpinnings behind the desire to free myself from the modern technological advancement of the microwave. Occasionally we busy Americans forget to take time to enjoy a meal and instead see food simply as fuel that is required to continue our mad dash toward our goals. I began to feel that if my life is so rushed that I need a microwave to expedite the preparation of my food, then I will continue to feel a sense of hurry while I am eating the meal. Whereas slowing down the pace of life by making time in your day to cook can naturally decrease your sense of feeling rushed, which can help reduce stress. This slower pace can, in turn, help you achieve a more calm mental state so that you can more mindfully enjoy your sustenance without rushing through it.

It is crucial to focus on the tasks at hand in the kitchen rather than multitasking. It is important to focus on cooking instead of simultaneously running back and forth between the kitchen, laptop, smartphone, errands, and chores. Perhaps life can be more satisfying when we are mindful while preparing to make our belly full. This mindfulness during the enjoyment of food can also help us avoid overeating since we will be consuming at a more thoughtful pace rather than stuffing our faces.

Around the time of these microwave musings, I turned thirty years old. I realized that I needed to make a greater effort to enjoy the simple joys of life. There will always be opportunities to earn more money, but earning back time is a bit more difficult. When you are always rushing through life with endless errands, tasks, shopping, gatherings, career advancement conquests, etc. you have much less time to appreciate an activity as simple as enjoying a meal. It can be so pleasant to savor each bite without your mind being preoccupied by the endless to-do list items that need to be checked off before bed.

I was dating a woman in her mid twenties who came over to hang out. She asked me why I did not have a microwave. My lack of this common appliance perplexed her. She did not understand my logic then proceeded to tell me this device is so convenient to heat up a cup of coffee in a minute. I responded "Exactly, you live a fast life... I don't want to rush through activities… I want to live a simple life… if you always rush through tasks then this can become a habit and you can become a rushed person in general." She was surprised by this response and let me know that she owned a microwave her whole life despite living in a poor country. I stated "You know what…

when we first met… you told me you were good at drawing… draw me an artistic picture of a microwave… I would rather have that than a real microwave."

Around the end of 2015 I was gifted two drawings. Both were on plain, letter size paper and done in pencil. One was a microwave with two eyes on top. This microwave had two arms - one on either side. One hand was opening the microwave door and another arm was holding a plate. The second drawing was a shiny microwave with a whole chicken inside. These works of art took time. She did not appear rushed while she drew them. It was as if she adopted a microwave-free life, but I doubt it. She simply enjoyed creating art much like I enjoy creating edible art that is my homemade cooking.

I was already living without a TV and microwave. The blender was next to go out the door. I used this appliance to blend hand pressed lime and lemon juice, grated ginger, and mint leaves in order to make my health elixir which I poured into an ice cube tray. I consumed one of these ice cubes with hot water each morning. The mint leaves were mostly for flavor. I felt that the real thirst quenching properties came from the citrus and ginger. Since I was trying to reduce my task list as well as the items on my shopping list, I was glad to take fresh mint off the list. Thus, it was easy enough to get rid of the blender.

As a general rule, I try to avoid processed foods. Some people believe canned food can be bad for the body. I prefer food that is fresh compared to food that somehow manages to stay around in an edible format for lengthy periods of time. However, I love sardines - which are generally canned. At most my canned food consumption was about one can of sardines a week. Fortunately for me, these little fish come in cans that have a tab to open the packaging. The can opener went out of my life as well.

Afterwards, I got rid of my rice cooker. I used this appliance several times a week. It was so convenient to set it and forget it. Then about fifteen minutes later the grain is warm, fluffy, and ready to eat. I was proud of how far I came in my goal of getting rid of most electronic possessions. But then I tried to cook rice in a pan. I thought you boiled the grain to cook it. It was ruined. Then I learned you have to put the right amount of water in a pan, bring it to a boil, then drop it to low heat. Basically grain is cooked by steam rather than boiling water. Thus, cooking grain without a rice cooker became too much of a burden to this aspiring minimalist. I admitted defeat and purchased another rice cooker.

Iron and ironing board were removed from my apartment. I wore the same few dress shirts and slacks to work each week. Every few weeks I would walk a few blocks from my place to have them dry cleaned. I spent two years on the road traveling for work and got enough zen of ironing done in hotel rooms to last a while.

Electric toothbrush was also tossed. I figured most of my life I used a traditional toothbrush and it seemed to work fine.

What was more important was to dedicate time to brush thoroughly rather than if the brush was electric or manual.

Even the wine glasses went out the door. I owned a couple of tulip glasses like those common in Belgium for their more elaborate and higher alcohol content ales. These sufficed for beer or wine.

The garlic press was also removed from my apartment. I could chop garlic on a cutting board.

I got rid of most electronics but the essentials. The thinking behind this decision to ditch most of my possessions was that by simplifying life, I could focus on trying to find joy outside of materialism and excessive consumption.

By this point, the only electronics I owned were a laptop, a smart phone, an old phone, and a rice cooker. Eventually I purchased a white noise machine because the surrounding area where I lived was excessively loud outside with the rooster, insane German shepherd, emergency vehicles and police helicopters passing by every hour. The summer of 2016 also led me to splurge on an indoor AC unit because the heat led to many consecutive sleepless nights, which was impacting my work. The apartment was furnished with a fridge and an oven. Washer and dryer were downstairs. By the time I left LA in mid 2017, I owned six possessions that plugged into an electrical outlet.

My apologies - I am forgetting one item, my personal favorite: a motion detection night light to plug into an electrical outlet in the bathroom for when I need to use the toilet in the middle of the night. This device, purchased at Walmart for a few dollars, has lasted years and is too great a possession to ditch in the name of minimalism. So it appears I owned seven electronic items. The internet modem brought the total up to eight. That about covers it.

In summary, I moved to DTLA during May 2015. The car was sold August 2015. I got rid of my can-opener September 2015 - at which point I quit eating canned food other than an occasional can of sardines or beer. The microwave was donated during November 2015 when I decided to avoid eating microwavable meals or using the device to heat food. I got rid of the electric blender in March 2016. I paid off the nearly $20,000 balance left on my college loans during April 2016, thereby becoming completely debt free. I even threw out my electric toothbrush August 2016. My iron and ironing board were given away December 2016. At the time of this writing - about two years after I left LA in mid 2017 - I still do not own the above mentioned items that I got rid of in Los Angeles, nor have I acquired many other replacement material possessions.

Chapter 20: He Was Surprised I Took Out Pomegranate Seeds By Hand - Meal Preparation As A Labor Of Love And Source Of Connection With The Natural World

While simplifying my life by discarding several material possessions, I also focused on reducing the complexity of my cooking and eating habits. Having only a few kitchen appliances and utensils helped keep meal preparation simple. Furthermore, a desire to eat as little processed, refined, or packaged foods as possible was another important factor in keeping my meals uncomplicated. For the sake of my health, I wanted to know what was in my food. So I thought it best to ensure that most food purchases were items that had only one ingredient - the item itself. But I also wanted variety to ensure I got plenty of vitamins and minerals as well as to avoid getting bored of eating similar foods most days.

Each weekend I would walk a few blocks to the nearest supermarket and purchase numerous items. Usually I would buy one of about thirty or forty different items. One carrot, one banana, one apple, one pear, one bag of grapes, one bunch of spinach, one potato, one tomato, etc. Then I would carry two giant bags for ten minutes on the walk back home. If I guessed, I would say that each hand carried about fifteen pounds of produce. I convinced myself I was strong enough to carry these awkwardly swaying thick plastic bags back to my apartment. When Whole Foods opened in DTLA at the end of 2015, my walk became twenty minutes each way. I never saw anyone else walking back to my poor neighborhood with paper bags with the Whole Foods logo. Perhaps people who shop at pricey markets have enough money to Uber back home. I saw the ten block walk as another form of exercise in terms of fitness and self-reliance.

Another factor that motivated me to purchase whole foods in their unadulterated state was that although I dined at many restaurants in and around LA and enjoyed some phenomenal dishes, I also paid for numerous meals that were subpar or came with rude service. I thought I could make my own delicious food without having to fork over my hard earned dollars to restaurants, their staff, and disrespectful waiters (who I heard can earn as much as I was making at my college required white collar job). I figured if I make a dish that does not turn out great at first, I have no one to blame but myself. And I will continue to learn, improve, and do better next time.

These are valuable lessons I did not want to miss by ignoring the importance of learning to cook for myself. It was important for me to grow as a person and create rather than always consuming the products of others.

As part of my simplified diet, I generally did not eat breakfast at home during the work week. Instead I would take fruit to work in a lunch box and eat some as a snack mid morning and mid afternoon. I had a box full of about a dozen varieties of nuts at work. These breakfast and lunch equivalents consisted mostly of fruits and nuts. At times I would have fruits with cheese and yogurt for breakfast, then fruits and nuts in the afternoon.

I cut fruits such as cantaloupe, honeydew, papaya, and watermelon. Peeling and cutting was required for fruits such as kiwi and mango. I would bring these items of produce to work in plastic containers. Some coworkers wondered if I cut and peeled these fruits myself, especially since items such as pineapple, cantaloupe, and watermelon can be purchased already cut up and on sale near the produce section at most grocery stores. During pomegranate season I would bring a container of pom seeds. Some folks inquired if I took all the seeds out by hand myself. Indeed, I took all the pomegranate seeds out manually. This surprised people. Perhaps our society is so busy that it does not seem appropriate for a white collar professional to spend his time taking out a hundred seeds from a pomegranate. But this is precisely the reason I felt the need to cut and peel my own fruit and take out all the pom seeds myself. We are so busy and so stressed, and here I found a way to be productive and exercise self-reliance while performing a task that was relaxing and reduced stress. After a long day at work staring at a screen and clicking away at a keyboard and mouse, it was refreshing to come home and cut fresh fruit for the following day's work snacks. I was able to get away from my computer and my smartphone, and focus on a task that I found to be meditative. It is wise to focus on the task at hand instead of multitasking when one is using a sharp knife to cut pieces of watermelon. In these modern times of endless demands that encourage most Americans to juggle several tasks at a time, it was a joy to focus on one activity at a time.

Did I ever care how long it takes to get all of the seeds out of a pomegranate? I don't think so. Perhaps it even takes a solid fifteen minutes. I actually like when it is pom season since I enjoy spending a few minutes once a week engaging in an activity with my hands that is completely different than what I do the rest of the week. Indeed, this is yet another benefit of getting a variety of produce that you have to cut, peel, and deseed yourself - you are using your hands differently than when you use your smartphone and computer. In an era when many people are addicted to mobile technology and experiencing health issues with their hands, wrists, neck, and mind, I found joy in using the muscles in my hands that I do not get to use most of the day. It made little sense to me to spend several dollars on a few pieces of cut up pineapple at the grocery store when I can get the whole one for cheaper, and get the joy of cutting it myself.

Since I was living, working, doing errands, and going to a gym all in DTLA, I did not see much of nature unless I would go beyond the city for a hike on the weekend. LA is a not a city known for its green spaces. Rather, the City of Angels is known for some of the worst urban sprawl in the US. The town has a serious lack of trees or natural greenery in any form. Even though Griffith Park and the Hollywood Hills area are close to DTLA, these areas are devoid of large trees. When hiking around these spots, you see the city and the sprawl and pollution and feel as if you are not in a natural setting. Spending most of my days in downtown brought a sense of nature-deficit disorder. Since I lived in areas where I could walk around some sort of natural setting until I moved to LA, I was desperate for nature. I began to find another joy in cutting and peeling produce as well as preparing and cooking whole food items. I felt blessed to be able to touch and feel nature even if it was briefly cutting up a watermelon or dicing a tomato. This is one of the reasons I learned to love taking out the seeds from a pomegranate. More time with nature if I cannot be in nature.

Each day when I walked home from work during my lunch break, and again after the day was over, I passed a typical scene around DTLA - the fruit cart vendor. This person stood by a silver cart with a rainbow umbrella. In the cart there was a bunch of ice with fruits sitting on top - usually watermelon, mango, pineapple, coconut, and some others. The fruit vendor cuts these fruits and sells pieces in plastic cups. On my walk home I would pass this laborer and think about how daily fruit cutting was an activity we shared in common.

Chapter 21: My Date Loved My $5 Home Cooked Meal More Than Dates Who I Have Taken To Expensive Restaurants, The Minimalism Cookbook, And How Budget-Friendly Eating Habits Led To The Best Health I Experienced In My Adult Life

Here is a sample of simple dishes that I incorporated as part of my minimalist lifestyle:

Generally speaking, I would use the rice cooker to prepare one of about a dozen varieties of grain. Then I would cook a vegetable or two such as spinach and mushrooms. The spinach would be cooked in hot water then the pan drained of liquid. I would set the spinach aside then saute the diced mushrooms in olive oil. Once this was completed, I would add the grain and cooked spinach back into the pan with the mushrooms and mix the ingredients together with a bit more olive oil and a hint of spice and black pepper.

This simple technique is how I create most of my meals. Given the amounts of grains I stored at home and the numerous varieties of produce I consumed each week, the possible combinations were plentiful. If I wanted a meal that was more Italian-ish I would cook sauteed diced eggplant, add a grain such as farro, and complete cooking the stir-fry-esque dish with a bunch of tomato or sun-dried tomato.

Stir-fry-esque meals more than three or four times a week can be a bit much. To add variety to the home cooked meals, I mixed up the routine by cooking a couple eggs and making a salad out of a few vegetables that I did not eat yet that particular week. Another day was for fried or boiled potatoes with other vegetables or a can of sardines. Employing this assortment of foods, I never felt like I lacked a variety of flavors and textures throughout the week. Thus, I was able to maintain a menu that was simple, healthy, filling, and inexpensive.

In general, I avoided cooking meat at home. I rarely craved meat during the week. A splurge meal or two of meat on the weekend was enough for my body. Perhaps my apartment was too small to cook meat. Perhaps I did not like heating up flesh in my own place for ethical reasons, yet I loved consuming it on the weekend. I was definitely not a vegetarian, but I tried to be conscious and mindful with regards to eating a previously living being. Perhaps this was beneficial for my health and wallet as a side benefit.

Rather than having hard and fast rules about aspects of life, such as diet, I tried to be flexible and listen to my body. I assumed that life will change, my body will change, and there will be a time that I can no longer eat foods that I loved and ate everyday. For example, people can develop allergies later in life. Humans can become ill and are no longer able to eat certain types of cooking such as fried food. Or we can develop ethical reasons to cut out certain foods.

Here is an example. I loved dried apricots since childhood. In LA, I met several Armenians. During April of each year, certain neighborhoods of LA which have a sizeable Armenian population will have cars flying the flag of this country. I first experienced this sight in an area called Altadena, which is a bit north of Pasadena. Sometime in April each year Armenians, the diaspora, and the Armenian communities abroad celebrate Armenian Genocide Remembrance Day to commemorate the killing of Armenians by the Ottoman Empire in 1915.

One day I was eating a dried apricot and I noticed the package said the dried fruit is from Turkey. I recalled noticing that most dried apricots I have eaten in the US come from Turkey. During this time I happened to be next to someone who I knew identified as Armenian. I asked this individual if they knew that most dried apricots are from Turkey. This person looked at me and with a serious face responded, "Yes, that's why I don't eat dried apricots."

Life will change our bodies and our minds in many unexpected ways throughout the course of our time on earth. When it comes to food and diet, it is important to listen to your body and to your heart. Therefore, it is crucial to make time to listen instead of rushing through life and multi-tasking our way through this journey without a moment to reflect.

Despite my general policy of not cooking meat at home, I did engage in this sinful activity on rare occasions. As a child growing up with immigrant parents, one of my favorite dishes was Uzbek Plov. Ukraine and Uzbekistan were once part of the Soviet Union so recipes get passed around. I cooked lamb in a pan. I added diced onions and garlic, and sauteed them in olive oil. Then I tossed some boiled carrot pieces and brown rice into the pan with the lamb, onions, and garlic. Finally I added the magic ingredient - golden raisins. After this, I stirred the ingredients around with a bunch of butter and black pepper. Divine.

I introduced this dish to a woman I was dating. She disliked lamb, but for some reason she loved this dish. Perhaps it's that magic ingredient. Who knew golden raisins can be combined with meat? I did. That is why I have loved this dish ever since I was a child. Feasting on this delight brought back fond memories of mother's cooking.

Another dish I first cooked in LA that is from the Motherland is a Russian style salad called vinaigrette. Russians and Ukrainians love beets. This red vegetable is a component of numerous Eastern European dishes. The staple soup of Russia, borscht, is red from beets. Many salads include beets. The salad I made required me to peel then boil beets, potatoes, and carrots. After draining the water, the root vegetables were cut into cubes. Then I added green peas, diced raw onion, and diced pickles. I mixed the items together with some olive oil (traditionally canola oil is used, but I do not like to have more than one oil at home to keep life simple). Cooking this easy dish for the first time made me feel like a true Ukrainian. Eating this refreshing salad, which is served cold, brought back pleasant memories of my younger years. Food tastes better when it is prepared with love.

I came across some folks eating carrot cake, which looked delicious. Part of me wanted a piece of the dessert but instead I pondered a way to make a dish that was similar yet healthy. So I grated some carrots and ginger. Then cooked steel cut oats in the rice cooker. Afterwards I moved these three items into a pan with melted butter and added some brown sugar, cinnamon, allspice, and nutmeg. All these ingredients were stirred together and cooked for a few minutes. Surprisingly the treat came out much tastier than expected. This meal was easy to make and required very little money and time. This is another illustration of how one can maintain a healthy body and mind in a society that has temptations at the office, grocery store, and around every other corner.

One time a woman I was dating came over for dinner. I cooked my signature "gypsy pizza." It was more of a risotto than a pizza, but I thought of it as a deconstructed pizza that was easy to make from scratch. Instead of rice I used amaranth. After cooking the specialty grain in a rice cooker, I transferred it to a pan, added pieces of mozzarella string cheese sticks and sun-dried tomatoes. I cooked these ingredients with olive oil until I got a rich and creamy risotto that tasted like pizza. She enjoyed this novel yet simple vegetarian dish. This woman never tried amaranth before. She thought the texture was similar to flying fish roe. These fish eggs are occasionally used as a garnish on some sushi rolls and are much smaller and finer than salmon caviar.

The pinnacle of my culinary innovation was inspired by a type of trash that I would see on the sidewalks in my neighborhood. On a regular basis, I noticed chewed up corn on the cob that was on a stick while walking around this part of DTLA. This rubbish came from people who would buy a common street food in Mexico and LA called elote, which is cooked corn on the cob covered in some sort of white condiment such as mayo, sour cream, or cotija cheese, then topped with spices like chili powder. This popular street food looks disgusting to me personally because I have an aversion to white colored condiments; but not white colored desserts. Sometimes the inedible parts of this street food were discarded on the street. After seeing all the neighborhood folk eating these elotes and tossing some of them onto the sidewalk, I was inspired to create a masterpiece culinary delight as an homage to the City of Angels. I bought some wooden skewers. Then I cooked a whole corn on the cob till it was gold to perfection.

Then I put little pieces of white chocolate onto the corn while it was in the pan so the heat could melt it and have it drip down the sides. I sprinkled cinnamon on top of the melted white chocolate. I served this dessert on a wood stick through the bottom. A woman I was dating and I feasted on this dessert that looked delicious. The taste was fantastic. I was hardly able to resist the urge to run outside of my apartment building and toss the leftover cob on a stick onto the sidewalk. Till this day I have never seen a restaurant make a dessert version of elote like the one I created. However, I was not in search of one elsewhere when I was able to make this fine treat at home.

Towards the end of 2015 when Whole Foods opened in DTLA, I was pleased because every other week it seemed that the produce section offered some sort of rare vegetable or fruit that was in season for a brief moment. For example, once I purchased a purple bell pepper. This was the first time I noticed such a veggie. These occasional surprises helped me to further stay engaged in my preparation and enjoyment of home cooked meals. I was particularly delighted when I went to get an eggplant while doing my shopping at Whole Foods and there was a variety I never saw before. This eggplant was not dark purple like a common eggplant nor was it long and skinny like a Chinese eggplant nor was it a small ball like a Thai eggplant. Instead, this eggplant was a slightly off-white creamy color and about the size of a softball, but more oval shaped. This eggplant looked like an egg that was a plant. I was shocked and wondered if this is how eggplants got their name. Or perhaps some scientists thought it would be punny to breed an eggplant that was white like an egg.

As my self-reliance via cooking at home continued, I experimented with various dishes. Some of which did not taste good, but this was part of the learning experience. I noticed that when I combined too many ingredients, a dish did not seem to come out as well. Perhaps the palate was overburdened with excess variety. I reflected on myself and life. When I am trying to perform too many tasks at once, I lose focus. When multitasking, I found that results are not as good as if I focused on one core function at a time before moving on to the next. For example, driving is fun but driving and texting is, according to some, as dangerous as drunk driving. Similarly, I found when there was too much going on in a dish because of a dozen ingredients, it can get overly complicated and lose its appetizing qualities. I even wondered if certain foods get processed by our bodies differently than others, and a dish with too many ingredients strains the body's digestion process and overall health. For me, it was an interesting thought. Overall, I felt it is best to maintain simplicity in life and in cooking. Cooking a grain or a potato or an egg and eating it with two or three vegetables was enough for me. This strategy kept my belly content and healthy.

I continued cutting and peeling fruit to eat at work, along with nuts that I kept in the office. A little bit of cheese and some yogurt paired well with fruit in the mornings. I kept eating a grain, potato, or egg along with some vegetables in the evening. I felt healthy and was able to avoid fatigue during work, even though I did not drink caffeinated tea or coffee.

My diet, regular swimming, other exercise, abstinence from alcohol, and only an occasional dessert kept me in great physical shape. At this point, I was the most lean since my early teenage years - and I was thirty years old at the time. During the healthiest few months of my time in LA I was the leanest male on the floor of the high rise building where I worked. The lack of processed food and refined sugar, combined with a challenging yet manageable job allowed me to feel productive during the day and tired in the evening, but not overburdened with worry after I left the office. This resulted in better sleep, which made resisting unhealthy food easier.

When I was at my most lean fitness, I noticed that the tiniest piece of junk food would cause a noticeable spike in stress. We rarely notice the increased tension that poor dietary choices have on our minds and bodies because for most Americans, our bodies are not running solely off a healthy variety of fresh produce, grains, and nuts. I even noticed the increase in lethargy and poorer sleep that came after I ate some salt or meat. I was happy not because I was the most slender of any point in my adult life, but rather because my body was functioning at the most optimal level of health and mental clarity that I experienced as an adult.

As I took time to listen to my body, reflect, and learn about the impact that diet and lifestyle choices were having on my health and wellness, I now continued with this simplified diet not for the sake of saving money to pay off college loans, but for the primary purpose of feeling my health was at the best that I have ever experienced. As an added benefit, my dietary choices and being involved in the food preparation process made me feel more independent, self-reliant, and resourceful. It felt empowering to not hand over my hard earned dollars to restaurants to complete tasks for me that I could do myself. I was grateful that I did not need to tip people whose job it was to carry food with a smile. A sense of joy came over me as I was able to cut out many companies and middlemen who are involved in getting an average American fed.

Chapter 22: He Played "Careless Whisper" While Sliding Across The Floor On His Back, Falling In Love With Jazz, And How Car Ownership Enables A More Complicated And Rushed Life

I knew that I could not live in DTLA for more than a couple years. So, despite my commitment to living on a low budget, I decided to make the most of my residential situation and appreciate as much about LA as I could before my time in this city ran out. Since I was living on about half of my income, I had room in my budget for arts and culture. After all, in addition to paying off my college loan, my second objective for the LA years was to learn to love America.

In November 2015 I received a message from a college friend who was living in New York City. He was working with a band who was going to be performing in LA soon. The jazz group was called Sammy Miller and The Congregation. I was keen to learn more about jazz because I was intrigued by its history and its improvisational aspects. Fortunately, the location where this group was playing was within a couple miles from my apartment at 1642 Bar in Historic Filipinotown.

I asked my friend about the price. He said free. That was music to my frugal ears. But the music was so good that I would have gladly paid. Apparently the show was free because some of the members of this group played at this bar when they were starting their musical careers long ago.

The show was more of a party than a performance. The venue was small but cozy. There was a total of eight musicians: drums, upright bass, piano, guitar, and four playing brass instruments.

At times the musicians would stand up on chairs while playing their instruments. Other times they would play at various places around the bar, including in the crowd. The highlight was when I saw one of the brass players slide across the floor on his back, pushing backward with his feet as he played "Careless Whisper" by George Michael. The drummer would take breaks from the drums to walk around the crowd and bang on tables and people's beer glasses with his drumsticks.

At one point, my head was leaning on the exposed brick wall while I was close to the woman I took here on a date. The smell of bergamot oil was radiating from her neck. Bergamot is what gives Earl Grey tea its distinct flavor. She applied oil derived from this fragrant citrus fruit earlier. My eyes were closed. Live jazz was playing a few feet from us. There was not much of a stage so it felt like we were part of the band.

It was bliss to see, hear, and feel the musicians using their hands, mouths, and bodies to create such pleasure for the crowd as they blew the brass, banged the drums, and caressed the strings. I enjoyed watching the musicians practicing an art they loved while exhibiting such passion and interacting with the crowd.

The jazz was invigorating. This exceptionally engaging performance may have been the first time I fell in love with jazz. I vowed to start exploring this staple of American culture.

Much to my chagrin, the woman that I was on a date with apparently did not feel the same way I did about this live jazz show. Instead of enjoying the show till the end, she had another agenda.

The band took a break at 11 p.m. The woman I was with told me she was eager to see a midnight showing of the 1974 comedy *Blazing Saddles* directed by Mel Brooks. The iconic film was being played at the independent theater New Beverly Cinema a few miles away. She said this was one of her favorite movies and that it was rare to see this classic film in theaters. I was disappointed to leave this phenomenal jazz show but she insisted we go to the movie. She drove us to the theater and the film lasted from about midnight to 2 a.m., which was late for someone accustomed to waking up at 5:30 a.m. during the work week.

On the drive home, she told me that Quentin Tarantino owned the independent theater where we saw the film, which was shown in 35 mm, and that this film was from his private collection. That additional background knowledge made this experience even more enjoyable for me.

I reflected upon the evening. After we left the jazz show for the theater, she was rushing and speeding and wondering if we would be late. This made me uncomfortable. One of the reasons I wanted to live car-free was to live simpler, slower paced, and with lower stress. When you have a car, you can squeeze many tasks into your day. As for me, I lived without a car for about four months by the time we went on this date. I learned that if I want to go out somewhere on a weekend night I can plan to get dinner and maybe one other activity. With a car-free life it would be unlikely that I would plan to go to several places in one night. Being car-free forces you to think about what you really want to prioritize with free time. This is actually better because the weekend entertainment and relaxation is much more enjoyable and low-stress. When you do only one or two activities, you can relax and enjoy yourself instead of having several items on that evening's to-do list. It's more enjoyable to have a mindful experience at one source of entertainment than experiencing a show while in the back of your mind thinking about needing to be at another event soon.

Unfortunately, all this mindfulness talk does not fly when starting to date someone new. It makes you look like you are unable to compromise.

The car-free life also allowed me to realize that it is better to get all your shopping done in one or two places than to go to several stores and spend all weekend doing America's favorite pastime - "errands." I eventually got all my groceries, soap, toothpaste, etc at Whole Foods. Target was for items like floss. And the nearby market was for gallons of spring water. It always amazed me when people would tell me that they need to get certain types of food at one store, other types at another store, and yet still more different types of food options at a third store. They said that certain groceries that are weekly staples in their home were cheaper at one store than another. I wondered if this was habit or if people have actually thought this through. Yes, body wash might be eight dollars at Whole Foods but four dollars at Target. However, it costs you probably two dollars in gas to drive from Whole Foods to another store to save two bucks. And I like to think that sitting in traffic or simply driving even if there is no traffic for an extra ten to twenty minutes does more harm for your health than saving two dollars. Besides, that bottle of body wash is going to last a month or two. It seems we add more stress to life in the form of driving around to save a few cents a day.

Some people spend an entire Saturday driving around to five different stores. When you are car-free you learn that the "convenience" of owning a car can lead to an inconvenient mental trap where a whole weekend day is spent feeling frustrated in store lines and dealing with rude drivers on the road. For me personally, I knew my time in LA was limited, so

I started enjoying the arts, culture, and entertainment rather than driving all over town doing errands and trying to consume too many experiences in one day.

Chapter 23: The Organ Was Used To Create Dog Barking Sounds For The Silent Film, The Symphony Played The Score To 'Casablanca,' Combing Live Music With Cinema At World Class Venues, The Pinnacle Of High Society, And How A Few Events Led To Loving American Cinema As A Source Of Budget-Friendly Cultural Appreciation Of My Adopted Country

I was disappointed to leave the passion-fueled jazz party by Sammy Miller and The Congregation early to see *Blazing Saddles* at Tarantino's theater. In retrospect, I am grateful the woman I was on a date with that night rushed us over to the theater because I got to see how passionate Angelenos are about film.

Later on I began dating another Angeleno woman who was also passionate about film. Being open to share her passion taught me a good deal about cinema.

In June 2016 I saw the iconic 1959 film *Some Like It Hot* at the Los Angeles Theater. The ticket was provided by the Los Angeles Conservancy as part of their Last Remaining Seats program. This was my first time at a historic movie palace. There are several movie palaces in DTLA. These palaces are not like the regular theaters of today. The Los Angeles Theater was built in the 1930s and has a seating capacity of about two thousand. Opulence characterizes the inside of the theater with its chandeliers and elegant wood designs throughout. Experiencing a film at such a movie palace is magnificent.

Since the seating capacity is so large, the line for this Saturday night showing was about two blocks long as it wrapped around the corner from the entrance. Each of these historic movie palaces in DTLA only plays a few films a year so these events are significant productions. People dress up fancy. Tours of the film projector room are given. Since I first toured the Los Angeles Theater I have noticed scenes in films and videos set at this movie palace and it brings me delight knowing that I experienced this exquisite venue in person.

Despite living in America for nearly thirty years this was my first time watching a movie with Marilyn Monroe. I was overjoyed with feelings of patriotism because I finally saw a film with one of the country's most famous stars. It was wonderful to watch such a film in a historic palace at the epicenter of the film industry. It was also wonderful to see a black and white film on the big screen. Lastly, I had zero clue that some of the film was set in my hometown of San Diego at the Hotel Del Coronado. I visited the Del ever since I was a young child, but was unaware that it was the setting of such an iconic film. About three weeks after seeing the film I visited San Diego and I stopped by the Hotel Del Coronado. Experiencing the hotel was different this time since I now had a greater appreciation for the landmark as part of American culture.

Two weeks after I experienced *Some Like It Hot* at the luxurious Los Angeles Theater, the woman I was dating got us tickets to another movie palace downtown - The Orpheum Theater. The Orpheum is also a grand movie palace built nearly 100 years ago. Perhaps its most incredible feature was the Mighty Wurlitzer organ.

At the Orpheum we watched the 1923 silent film *Safety Last!* I was shocked when the Wurlitzer organ came up out of the ground on stage. This was not only my first time seeing a silent film, but I was seeing it in a magnificent theatre. In addition, *Safety Last!* at the Orpheum was my first time hearing the organ as a soundtrack to a movie. It was fantastic. All of the sound for the entire film was created by the organ. The most memorable part of this movie was when the dog was barking but since it was a silent film the man playing the organ made barking sounds with the instrument. I was awe-inspired by this experience and was overwhelmed with joy that this woman introduced me to classic film. LA was the perfect place to start becoming passionate about cinema.

In November 2016 we went to the architectural marvel that is the Walt Disney Concert Hall in DTLA and saw the 1942 classic film *Casablanca*. The score was played by the LA Symphony. This was my first time seeing a movie with the music played by nearly one hundred musicians live. We were in about the fifth row. It was a one of a kind experience to feel the intense energy of a film and see the faces of the nearly one hundred people creating music in front of you. Watching a film with a symphony playing the score allows the viewer to witness the magnificent human talent used to create sounds that evoke powerful emotions, such as suspense. This is especially true for concert halls that invest heavily in acoustics. After experiencing a film with a symphony playing the music I began to appreciate film scores; even when watching a movie at home. For these reasons I highly encourage everyone to experience a film with live symphony once in their lifetime, even though this particular lesson in arts appreciation cost $182 a ticket. Fortunately, most large cities that have an orchestra will show historic films with the score played live; and most will probably be less expensive than in LA.

After seeing *Casablanca* with the symphony I even took an interest in learning more about movie score composers, thereby, discovering Bernard Hermann. He composed scores for iconic films with signature sounds such as *Vertigo* and *Taxi Driver* as well as the historically significant movies *Psycho* and

Citizen Kane. Taking time to appreciate how music can be used to create a psychological symptom as in the case of *Vertigo* resonated powerfully with me and led to richer and deeper experiences with cinema.

My growing appreciation for film scores led to an interest in classical music. Before this point I thought classical music was only for elderly or aristocrats.

In December 2016 I came back to the Walt Disney Concert Hall for a classical music performance by the LA Philharmonic. The show was titled Dudamel and Russian Masters. Gustavo Dudamel was the conductor and the musical pieces played came from Rachmaninoff, Prokofiev, and Scriabin. We had good seats so I wanted to ensure I could appreciate the show. Up until this point I possessed zero knowledge of classical music. Thus, the day before the show I watched the 1984 film *Amadeus* about Wolfgang Amadeus Mozart. I was advised this was an approachable movie for a two and a half hour introduction to classical music.

Before leaving LA in June 2017, I had one last experience at a movie palace. In early March 2017 we went back to the Los Angeles Theater to watch the 1962 classic film *What Ever Happened To Baby Jane?* This event was full of people dressed fancy and I was once again surrounded by the elegance of this luxurious historic theater. The film was exceptional. By this point I saw a few black and white films on the big screen that year. I used to think black and white films were pointless and outdated. I would never watch them.

However, by being open minded to new experiences I was able to develop a greater appreciation for classic film. From that time on, I began watching classic films on my own. I learned to love Hitchcock films, Clark Gable films, Woody Allen movies, old school Westerns, and on and on. My ignorance kept me in the dark from cultural joy but I was woke now. A whole new world was opened up. The history buff in me was grateful for this new found aspect of American culture. Watching classic films such as *Vertigo* allowed me to see what mesmerizing cities like San Francisco looked liked many decades ago. It was like going to a historic photo gallery but the pictures were moving.

During December 2016 I watched the 2011 film *The Artist*. This film is essentially a modern silent movie about silent films. The lead actor is a famous star of silent films but then in the late 1920s talking pictures ("talkies") start to dominate the film industry. The actor is unable to adapt to the new technology. He then spirals into the depths of despair. *The Artist* was one of my favorite movies that I saw during those two years in LA. It wonderfully depicts life in the heart of the Los Angeles film industry during one of the greatest transformations experienced by that industry. Some of the scenes were shot at places I visited in LA such as the Bradbury Building as well as some of the movie palaces. One of the scenes shows a silent film being viewed with the score played by an orchestra. I was glad to have had a similar experience with *Casablanca* and the LA symphony. There was even a scene at what appeared to be the Orpheum Theater where people were watching a silent film. Visiting the Bradbury Building, seeing a film with orchestra, and seeing a silent film at a movie palace were activities I enjoyed before seeing *The Artist*. These experiences allowed me to have deeper relatability to the film, which increased my appreciation for this cinematic work of art.

Furthermore, I was advised that watching a real silent film (without organ) before seeing *The Artist* would make it more enjoyable. Charlie Chaplin's *City Lights* was the recommended silent film. This was my first time seeing a Chaplin film. It provided insight into how actors communicated with exaggerated eye movements and body language when voice was unavailable. In addition, years later I finally saw the iconic 1950s film *Singin' in the Rain*, which gave further perspective on the technological innovation that replaced silent films with talking pictures.

In the two years that I lived in LA from 2015 to 2017, I experienced two cultural highlights. The first was seeing a silent film at a grand historic movie palace where the sound to the entire film was created by a musician playing an organ. The second was watching a film at the world class Walt Disney Concert Hall with the score played by a symphony. Both shows combined film with live musical instruments. I like to think of these two types of events as the peak of "high society." These two experiences opened my mind to the joy and beauty of cinema, which helped me develop a greater appreciation of American culture.

Chapter 24: Live Jazz As A Budget-Friendly Way To Appreciate American Culture

The night I experienced the energetic musical performance of Sammy Miller and The Congregation as well as the film *Blazing Saddles* was joyous for two reasons - jazz and film. Before LA I did not know much about jazz. A previous coworker who was a musician told me that the roots of jazz came from slavery in America. Then in 2008 I started studying craft beer - even reading lengthy books on the topic. Back in those days there weren't several thousand breweries in America. One of the original craft breweries that I enjoyed around this time was Dogfish Head out of Delaware. The brewery offered a beer called Bitches Brew named after a Miles Davis album. I remember seeing a video online where the founder was talking about this beer and how the jazz of Miles Davis inspires the creativity at Dogfish Head. I did not learn much more about jazz till years later, but these two brief encounters planted a seed that took a bit of time to sprout.

After experiencing Sammy Miller and The Congregation in LA and seeing how lively and improvisational a musical performance can be, I began to understand that live music at intimate venues can be an engaging and participatory experience. Researching another intimate jazz venue led me to the Blue Whale in Japantown, DTLA. I came here in January 2016 and saw a trumpeter and his band. The performance was a show rather than a party like Sammy Miller. Nonetheless, I was glad to have a cozy club that held weekly jazz shows near my residence.

To continue my jazz self-education I watched the 2014 film *Whiplash*. This movie solidified my growing affinity for jazz. Even though some musicians may find the film overly dramatic, it was still a good introduction. A few days after seeing *Whiplash* I went back to the Blue Whale. The event I saw at this location in March 2016 was eye-opening. At one point the drummer pulled out a vase with a spherical base about the size of a bowling ball, which appeared ceramic, and was about two feet high. He put the opening of the vase to the microphone and began using it to make sounds. This experience enlightened me to jazz as a source of helping people become more open-minded. I noticed jazz was a bit like life. Sometimes random occurrences show up in your life and you go with the flow and try to appreciate it, even if this is the first time you hear a ceramic vase played as an instrument.

As my interest in jazz grew I wanted to experience other activities distinct to LA. One of the most iconic buildings in LA is the Walt Disney Concert Hall. Now that I was becoming a patron of the arts, I wanted to see a musical performance at this venue. Fortunately for me, a jazz group called Mack Avenue was having a show at Walt Disney during April 2016. I figured for a jazz group to play at such a renowned venue, they were probably very talented. Seats up front were significantly costlier than a twenty dollar show at the Blue Whale. So I got a $46 ticket up in the nosebleed section - technically called the Balcony Level. I got to see a show at this venue but I did not fully experience the energy of the musicians because I was so far away at this concert hall with over two thousand seats.

During April 2016 I went on a date to Catalina Jazz Club a couple blocks or so from the epicenter of Hollywood Boulevard. I yearned to see some smooth jazz and the artist that night was saxophonist Kim Waters. The venue was small-ish and relatively intimate but still big enough that the seating capacity was about 200 people. We got to the venue early to get a good seat up front. Kim Waters played some great smooth jazz. The music was sensual, soft, and upbeat. This event was special because he was not only a great musician, but a hilarious entertainer. The night was full of laughs and plenty of sexually suggestive comments. Perhaps that can happen sometimes when a man's life work is creating music that some say is an aphrodisiac. And the crowd at this restaurant music venue was equally entertaining since some were quite vocal and engaging with the musicians. I was new to live music so I found it fun to be surrounded by such a lively and interactive crowd as well as such an entertaining artist who was at times comedic despite the seriously astounding sax he played.

One morning during April 2016, I walked to the center of DTLA to buy groceries. It was still early so the city lacked its usual car and foot traffic. I noticed an African American male who looked about sixty years old wearing a suit and playing a trumpet. He played well so I listened for a while. We ended up chatting. He told me about a music venue that was a great spot back in the day called The Baked Potato. A few months later I found my way there per the recommendation of this artist.

In July 2016 I went to one of the coolest bars with live music in DTLA called Clifton’s. The establishment has three floors inside and several different themed rooms as if it were a few bars and lounges under one roof. One of the rooms provided live music on occasion. The night I came to experience Clifton's the live band consisted of two sax players, a drummer, upright bass player, a banjo player and a female singer. The music was more swing but my recent learnings of jazz made it easy to appreciate other genres of music that included sax and were upbeat. As an added bonus, the musicians and many of the patrons were dressed from the swing era of the 1920s and 1930s. I approached this genre with an open mind, and was grateful to be learning more about American history, arts, and culture.

Later on in July 2016 I met up with a college friend who was going to see a show at the massive open air theater, The Hollywood Bowl. She had an extra ticket for me. I was glad for the new cultural experience and to visit a new venue. The group was called Galactic, a funk and jazz band from New Orleans. This was my first time hearing funky jazz live. It was extremely upbeat and fast paced compared to the other styles of jazz I heard before.

The Hollywood Bowl is an amphitheater in the Hollywood Hills with a view of the Hollywood sign far off in the distance. It is representative of LA in some ways. There are private-esque seating areas up front where the rich people sit. Some of these wealthy folk have season passes and go to all these events at this outdoor theater. Then there is the rest of society. We were about mid way up. But the Hollywood Bowl is cool because you can bring your own alcohol and food.

However, with a capacity of nearly 17,000 this venue is hardly intimate, and much larger than the small environments I prefer. I like being close enough to see the musicians sweat and their facial expressions. At the Hollywood Bowl we could see the musicians up close on the big screen tv to the side of the stage. Otherwise, the artists looked as big as ants. But it was cool to experience the Hollywood Bowl at least once.

As we were sipping alcohol that we brought in and enjoying Galactic's performance, my friend was schooling me on this type of music. She told me about Dr. John and his ragtime piano playing. She said piano is the most true of all instruments because each key is so sensitive in so many ways, whereas the guitar is much more limited. These may be just opinions, but I was grateful for any insights that served as a starting point for further research. Besides, I never heard of the term "ragtime" before.

I was intrigued by ragtime. So I watched a made-for-TV film called *Scott Joplin* from 1977 about one of the greatest ragtime musicians in American history. The history buff in me enjoyed learning about this early 1900s genre of music that was highly influential to the development of jazz. I especially enjoyed the dueling piano scene in an early 1900s brothel where it is said that this style of music originated. It was cool to gain perspective on how different genres of music evolve and influence one another over time. I enjoyed gaining a greater appreciation for the subtleties of human progress.

About a week after seeing a show at the Hollywood Bowl, I went to LA's other main outdoor venue - The Greek Theater in Griffith Park. The capacity here is nearly 6,000 so it is a bit more manageable to experience a show here compared to the stadium-like Hollywood Bowl. We came here to see Chris Botti. Up until this point I did not know who Botti was but as I was learning about jazz I played a song to a woman I was dating called *Miles and Miles of Miles Davis* by Malcolm McLaren who my mother used to listen to while I was a kid. I told her I loved the trumpet in this song and she said Chris Botti plays like that. So I looked him up and noticed he was playing in LA soon. Another benefit of living in LA is that pretty much whatever you want can be had there. Shortly after that we went to see him at the Greek Theater.

The show was marvelous. His trumpet playing was indeed intense and beautiful. He came down into the giant crowd on occasion and blew his horn into the face of some of the viewers. Botti is a top-notch trumpeter. So I was surprised when they announced the other musicians. As the pianist was introduced I thought I recognized him. The guy playing piano for international trumpeter Chris Botti at a massive amphitheater was the same guy I saw playing piano at the Blue Whale - a small jazz club that fits about a hundred people comfortably. I believe the pianist's name was Geoffrey Keezer. It was delightful to hear all this live music and to learn about this art form and industry.

A tour of LA's jazz clubs continued when we went to Pips On La Brea in October 2016. This venue is down in Mid City about four miles south of Hollywood. The jazz there was calmer than other shows I saw in LA up to this point. There was a drummer, a bass player, and older gentleman playing sax inside. It seemed that most of the patrons were outside on the patio. While that made me feel that jazz was losing popularity we did get a good seat up front. I smiled when the group started playing the Pink Panther theme song.

Exploring LA's jazz venues continued with a stop at The Baked Potato, which has been around since the 1970s. This establishment is located one block from the subway station for Universal Studios Hollywood. The live music that night in

October 2016 was a bluesy jazz. This fusion music was funky. The guy on the keys was bald with long hair, the guitarist looked like Michael Moore, and the drummer wore a biker style outfit with his leather vest and white bandana. The saxophonist played with passion; it was as if he was making love to his instrument. This venue might have been one of the coolest live music spots I visited to up to this point. The way the band was playing, combined with the distinctiveness of the venue made the show feel more like a jam session in someone's garage rather than an actual entertainment establishment. It felt as if there was much more room for experimenting and improvisation at this venue than somewhere more sophisticated, like the Blue Whale in downtown. Even the layout of the establishment felt like a grungy garage (I say that in the most complimentary way possible) because of the decor and the way all the seats were so crammed together and so close to the stage. I am unsure more than fifty spectators could fit in this place at a time, which added to the intimate environment. The sign in the front said the group playing that night was Don Randi and Quest.

The price for an experience at The Baked Potato was reasonable. The show was about twenty dollars with the understanding that two items should be purchased; but you can simply buy a cup of tea and dessert for another ten bucks rather than two glasses of wine for approximately twenty five dollars.

I came back to the Blue Whale again during January 2017. This venue allowed me to become more open-minded about jazz and art in general. Instead of a drummer pulling out a ceramic vase to make sounds, a singer got on stage and started performing spoken poetry and creating sounds as if he was the various jazz instruments played that night. This experience helped me learn to appreciate a new approach to art.

A date and I drove to Ventura to check out a music venue called Squashed Grapes that I found out about while living there during early 2015. The intimate venue seated about fifty people. Squashed Grapes makes their own wine in the venue so you get to try artisan wine at inexpensive prices while getting to experience some cool musical acts from the area. I like going to these cozy jazz spots because you can see some music for maybe no more than twenty dollars a person. I prefer to see a musician sweat and see their facial expressions and watch them experiment rather than spending hundreds of dollars to see a star. Seeing a big name can be good on occasion, but it is more entertaining and budget friendly for me to experience up and coming talent. In addition, it is less stressful to be able to show up to a venue at a moment's notice than to plan for a show weeks in advance.

At Squashed Grapes that night in April 2017 the group consisted of a saxophonist, guitar player, bass player, and drummer. When I lived in Ventura during 2015 I visited this venue and saw a female who was blind playing the flute exceptionally well. That was an awe-inspiring experience and seeing such hidden gems keeps me coming back to small venues. In contrast, we saw AFI perform at the Wiltern Theater in LA's Koreatown during February 2017. The seating capacity at this theater was nearly 2,000. When AFI started the whole building was shaking like an earthquake.

Seeing music at a smaller venue is closer to my view of life. A musician has a goal, works toward that point, but along the way might make a mistake. Perhaps someone in the crowd will notice the mistake or wonder why the artist made a strange facial expression. The musician might mess up a note, but they pick themselves up and move forward. They may even decide to improvise as they embrace a feeling in the moment, which can lead to a result that is different than the initial goal but still beautiful; and possibly even more splendid because the improvisation allowed for the freedom to incorporate an intense feeling. You begin to see that life is not about the survival of the fittest - it is about the survival of those that can best adapt. You also realize the journey is more important than the destination. This is what makes live music such a worthy and soul enriching experience. Especially when I can see the faces the musicians make that provide insight into how much effort has gone into a song. It is a joy being close enough to the musicians to see them communicate with eye contact while they advise one another on the direction of the improvisation. A little burst of delight travels through my neural pathways when I see a trumpeter letting the saliva come out of his horn and splatter on the stage as he takes a break while the other musicians continue to jam. At this proximity to the musicians I can see a bass player embracing, caressing, tenderly massaging, swaying, and dancing with his curvy, wide-hipped instrument more passionately than he would with a lover. It is enthralling to feel the music in my heart when I listen with my ears.

Shortly before leaving LA during mid 2017 I watched the 2016 film *La La Land*. I was hesitant to watch it at first because I thought I had an aversion to musicals. But the film did a great job conveying the significance of jazz. It turns out many people loved this film and it won top awards. In this movie, there is a mention of The Baked Potato jazz club. During May 2017 we went to the Baked Potato again. The venue seemed more crowded now and the patrons appeared more sophisticated than the folks who came to this jam session garage-like venue months before *La La Land* came out. I got one pour of Lagavulin which cost twenty two dollars. That is about one third the price of the bottle and not what I expected to pay at a music spot with a divey feel. But the establishment was now mentioned in a critically acclaimed film. Furthermore, since we did not come early to this jazz club, there was only standing room left during the show. However, the silver lining is exactly what the film hoped to achieve - get more people interested in this genre of music.

Chapter 25: A Turkish Tourist Helped Me Develop A Fondness For Architecture

Along with cinema and live music, particularly jazz, my two years in LA helped me learn to appreciate another form of art - architecture. My initial encounter with architecture was somewhat accidental.

During August 2015 I was walking home from work and saw a beautiful woman. I asked if she wanted to get coffee. She said "Now?" I replied, "My wallet is at home but I can meet you in thirty minutes." She stated "Let's go for a walk."

This female tourist told me she was a Turkish immigrant and European national. The skin of her petite frame was a caramel color. She was from a French speaking part of Europe and spoke with a lovely accent. She wanted to find the Bradbury Building and informed me it is the oldest building in LA. Apparently this historic landmark was built in 1893. I had little interest in historic buildings before. But now that this gorgeous woman was interested, I was keen to maintain her company so I developed an interest in architecture during that moment. We chatted about being immigrants and international travels. Finally, we arrived at the Bradbury. I passed by it a dozen times but never noticed it. The marvelous interior of the Bradbury had a beautiful atrium, staircases, walkways, and elaborate ironwork, which has been featured in many films such as *Blade Runner* and *The Artist*. She took a bunch of photos and asked me to take several of her.

Another historical landmark that she wanted to see was the Angels Flight - a funicular on about three hundred feet of inclined railway connecting the flat area near Grand Central Market to the top of Bunker Hill. When we got to Angels Flight I invited her over for dinner and asked if she has ever eaten Ethiopian food. I told her that I recently picked up some injera from Little Ethiopia and could prepare some food to go along with it. I inquired if she knew what injera was. She said “The crepe thing?” Yes, I suppose if you are French then injera can look like a sourdough crepe. She said she had plans with friends for dinner. We spent about forty minutes together. I was mesmerized by her architecture much more than the beauty of the Bradbury Building. However, she then mentioned a comment about her boyfriend back home. I said it was time for me to head home. She asked if I was interested in going to Universal Studios with her. I replied maybe.

Later that day, I went for a swim downtown. I saw a woman at the gym who recently came over for dinner. She gave me a ride home after our workout. We hung out for a bit in my apartment. On her way out she walked past my kitchen and noticed the injera on the counter and says "Ahh, so you got a big tortilla." Sure, if one is Hispanic, I suppose it does look like a sourdough tortilla. Simple exchanges can brighten your day.

I was grateful for accidentally stumbling upon an interest in architecture simply because I went along with a woman to some place she probably found in a guide book. This encounter with a stranger that led me to admire the beauty that I passed many times without noticing was a learning experience. This was another reminder that while you are busy making plans to see the world and travel to dozens of countries, busy thinking about meeting friends in the future, endlessly thinking about how to climb higher in one's career, or constantly checking smartphones, you are too preoccupied to notice the wondrous joys right in front of you. We can enrich our life with more delight if we take a few minutes to slow down the pace from our momentum-filled days to appreciate the present.

Since LA has so much sprawl, there are a lot of buildings. Nature and the ability to marvel at its wonder is lacking when you live and work in DTLA. The inaccessibility of natural landscapes led me to develop a fondness for the beauty of architecture to fill this void. A band aid to heal from nature-deficit disorder. I learned to appreciate the beauty created by man when I was unable to cherish the enchantment created by the divine powers of the world.

Visiting architectural marvels such as the Walt Disney Concert Hall allowed me to appreciate another element of American art. Frank Gehry's masterpiece is the most stunning building in LA County. Giant silver metallic sails of various shapes, sizes, and curvatures flow in all directions. The building looks completely different depending on the angle from which one observes this gigantic work of art. Learning to value architecture helped me love the place where I am rather than believing "there is better, where we are not" (my word for word translation of a Russian saying that basically amounts to the grass is greener on the other side).

During April 2016 I visited one of superstar architect Frank Lloyd Wright's best preserved pieces in LA - The Hollyhock House. This architectural gem and historical landmark built in the 1920s is located near Thai Town and Hollywood and was a few stations away from my place by subway. Taking time to wander around the house and property provided me with a chance to cherish the minute detail that goes into creating an architectural masterpiece. All the smallest details about the layout, designs, angles, shapes, materials, colors, and Mayan-esque motifs were all carefully thought about in the artist's vision. I gained an understanding that architecture can create a building where the whole is greater than the sum of the parts.

In May 2016 I visited Pasadena to learn about Craftsman homes, which were part of a movement in American home design from the early 1900s. Craftsmans remain highly regarded, with many such homes typically well preserved. Craftsman homes were built before the post World War II economic expansion and the resulting wave of suburbanization, which included the development of large housing communities with cookie-cutter home designs. Some of these communities with their fancy sounding names might have about five home designs for an area that includes five hundred homes. So every few homes the design scheme is repeated. On the other hand, Craftsmans tend to look more individualized, especially because they were not mass-produced to the degree of modern day homes.

One of the most iconic American Craftsman homes is The Gamble House in Pasadena. This beautiful mansion built in the first decade of the twentieth century is a historic landmark and a museum with public tours. Every feature of the house and furnishings were custom designed. Touring this property was another opportunity to learn to appreciate every detail about a piece of architecture as a work of art. The various types of wood used throughout the house had zero knots exposed, which is extremely extravagant. That was probably the most interesting fact that I remember from the tour. The owners of the Gamble House were so wealthy, and the forests in the Western US were still so abundant this zero knot on exposed wood was still possible. I remember this sticking in my head for a long while after my visit. Whenever I was in a house where I noticed a knot in the exposed wood I would chuckle to myself. I thought to myself how relatively poor this person was even though they believed they were wealthy.

Another interesting fact about the Gamble House is that two USC School of Architecture students live in the house. These students change each year. I imagine these are probably the most gifted of all the students in the program. I am unaware that I have ever been in a culturally or historically significant place where gifted folks had the privilege to live inside.

At the time of my visit there was one other feature about the house that was novel. There were two swords hanging on the wall. Both from the Civil War. One from the Confederate Army and another from the Union forces.

The Gamble House was also Doc's home in the 1985 hit movie *Back to the Future*.

After The Gamble House I walked about two miles east to an historic district called Bungalow Heaven. This area features several hundred Craftsman homes. I wandered around numerous blocks taking in the visual beauty, noticing the subtle differences, and being amazed by the craftsmanship of these bungalow homes from the early 1900s. It was impressive to see ordinary people preserving these specimens of history in this neighborhood that felt like an open-air museum.

I was grateful to learn about the significance of Craftsmans because my hometown of San Diego has a neighborhood called North Park, which is designated a Historic Craftsman Neighborhood. On a visit to San Diego after my wanderings around Bungalow Heaven I strolled North Park with a newfound appreciation for the many homes in this area designated San Diego Historical Landmark buildings. Before these architectural insights I simply associated this hipster-filled neighborhood as the epicenter of SD's craft beer scene. Speaking of craft beer, one of the first craft breweries that I liked was called Craftsman and they were out of Pasadena. I did not know of the connection to the homes at that time. But many craft breweries pay homage to what makes their hometowns special and this would not be the first time I learned fun facts about a locale from the name of a brewery or the names of their beers. When my genuine thirst for knowledge leads to random connections, it's as if a little pinch of delight is sprinkled onto my day.

With plenty of daylight left I continued my self-guided walking tour of the city famous for its Rose Parade. The nearly one hundred year old Pasadena City Hall is a stunning work of architecture. As I was strolling around this municipal building I noticed two giant black heads on the ground. These heads were about ten feet tall and if I could crawl into them, the space inside could fit about five of me. The two enormous heads were sculptures of Jackie and Mack Robinson as a memorial to great athletes from this area. The artistic memorial provides a history of the brothers, which was especially beneficial for me because I was not versed on the significance of these gentlemen before this point.

Back in June 2016 we watched a silent film at The Orpheum. When we walked out I noticed the big turquoise monster of the concrete jungle. The building takes up half a city block but isn't much higher than a dozen stories, so it is more stocky than the financial skyscrapers. Built around the 1930s The Eastern Columbia Building is one of the most remarkable buildings in DTLA, along with the Walt Disney Concert Hall. This sea-green giant is considered one of the finest specimens of Art Deco architecture in the world. Easily the most colorfully striking building in downtown, it includes a four sided clock at the top that is a few stories high. The sharp design work and striking patterns of the gold trim that can be seen from the sidewalk was enchanting. Intrigued by this architecture, I began to research Art Deco - an art movement from the early 1900s. Accidentally running into beauty by simply noticing my surroundings, which made LA great, led to some joy-filled learnings. I began to see that Art Deco was not simply about architecture but included all kinds of design. It even had its own font-types characteristic of the style; just like the Craftsman movement. I was extremely thankful for the hard work and efforts of the Los Angeles Conservancy. Similarly, I was appreciative of the many people behind the preservation of historically significant art that budget-minded folks such as myself can derive much joy and inspiration from by simply being in the presence of such a gargantuan tower.

Appreciation of the Eastern Columbia Building led me to stop and stare when I was walking back home from Koreatown. Standing before me was a building that looked like a little cousin of the Eastern Columbia, which was called the Bullocks

Wilshire. Both of these buildings were opulent, striking, and beautiful.

Taking an interest in architecture allowed for a greater appreciation for the simple pleasures in life. Watching the 2013 film *The Great Gatsby* was more enjoyable because so much of the art and design was Art Deco, a style for which I grew a great fondness by the time I saw the movie. In addition, I would be walking down a random street in a city other than LA, and notice a small-ish building a few stories high that might seem like an average older office building to most. Then I would notice the motifs and the inspiration from Art Deco. A happy smirk lands on my mug because knowledge of history and style makes the everyday occurrence more enjoyable. A touch of gratitude without spending a dime.

The last place I visited on my LA architecture tour was The Greystone Mansion, which occurred during July 2016. I heard this home served as a film location for countless movies, including one of my personal favorites - *There Will Be Blood* (2007). It is commendable that the city of LA and groups of its residents are adamant to preserve historical landmarks for the enjoyment of all. The grounds were beautiful and it was a great way to spend a few hours in the peaceful atmosphere, especially to get away from the chaos of downtown. Preparation for a wedding on the grounds was taking place so I was able to hang out by a harp player practicing her angelic instrument. This was likely my first time being in such proximity to a harp player. The music was truly divine.

My final experience with architecture in LA is one that lasted the entire two years I lived downtown. I worked next door to the Wilshire Grand, which became the tallest building in Los Angeles when it was completed mid 2017. The side of the building where I worked faced the construction. I experienced all the not-so heavenly sounds that came with the construction of a ginormous seventy three story skyscraper. Seeing this enormous structure rise slowly day-by-day made me respect the effort that goes into making buildings like the Eastern Columbia. My lungs were definitely a victim of this building's construction since I walked home past heavy duty trucks parked out front regularly. For some reason they kept their engines idling as I walked past breathing in diesel exhaust fumes.

Chapter 26: A Painting Covered In Elephant Shit - Embracing The Budget-Friendly Personal Growth And Zest For Life That Develop Through Spending Time In Art Museums

LA is a world class city with countless cultural amenities. I vowed to take advantage of this opportunity by visiting the city's art museums. Before moving to LA around age thirty, I visited this city only a handful of times. In my teens my mother took us to visit The Getty - a massive complex in the mountains near Santa Monica. During that visit I climbed around the buildings and structures. I have zero recollection of seeing any art during that visit. Now that I was older, I was able to appreciate the art at this world renowned museum. I never took any art history classes in high school or college, so I started teaching myself by visiting various art museums. Furthermore, I traveled to numerous countries, saw the architecture and sights of the old world, and learned about European culture. This context gave me some background to appreciate the works of art in the museum. For example, artists from centuries ago loved to paint images of Venice. I felt a greater appreciation for these old world paintings after I visited this Italian city. In another example, I had more context to admire a painting of a bullfight by Francisco Goya after I learned about this famous artist at the Museo del Prado in Madrid, and experienced his collection of works called *The Black Paintings*. Reading Hemingway's book on bullfights, *Death in the Afternoon,* and seeing a bullfight in Mexico City provided further context to cherish the painting.

The Getty offers splendid views of Century City and the smog engulfing DTLA. The grounds have beautiful gardens and architecture. My visit here was a great way to spend several hours that day in October 2015.

Museums in most cities are generally not cost prohibitive. I reckon the average museum in LA cost about twenty dollars, which is a valuable use of scarce resources, considering most museums provide at least two or three hours of learning and entertainment. Some museums are free. Despite being on a budget, it was safe to spend about eight dollars an hour on expanding my mind so that I could continue my journey of self improvement. Sometimes I would take fruits and nuts in my backpack and eat them at the museum. There were times that I would take long rides on crowded buses to and from museums. Eventually I became less frugal and would spend nearly ten dollars to Uber rather than dealing with LA buses to save seven dollars. But it took a long time before I adopted this luxurious standard of living.

Some museums were walking distance. One such cultural institution was The Museum of Contemporary Art (MOCA) in DTLA. I visited in November 2015. Since the focus here was on contemporary works rather than the mostly historic pieces at The Getty, I was able to expand my horizons about the possibilities of art. There was a work of art that really puzzled me. A large canvas stood on the ground rather than being hung on the wall. It was probably taller than me and several feet wide. An artistic image of a monkey holding a vase was on the canvas. Above the vase were three large brown clumps bigger than baseballs. They were three dimensional and popped out of the canvas. Titled "Monkey Magic - Sex, Money, and Drugs" - this work from 1999 was created by Chris Ofili of England. The three spheres above the vase and the two similar spheres on which the artwork was standing were made out of elephant dung. The description stated that the artist born to Nigerian parents wanted to create a satirical piece based on racist stereotypes "giving viewers what they 'want from black artists' - voodoo kings, drug dealers, and the element of the exotic."

As the years progressed, I visited several dozen museums and this was the only time I saw shit displayed. I saw that art could be used to challenge convention as well as serve political purposes. Perhaps most importantly, art allows one to gain more insight into humanity and the experience of others in this world. This "shitty" work of art was not so shitty for my studies of the human condition. There was also art conveying the difficulties of homosexuals striving to reach equality. This was not your typical beauty of old-world masters depicting religious figures and royal persons. In addition to art related to racial issues, I was also exposed to innovative American painters such as Mark Rothko and Jackson Pollock. I noticed that paintings by these two artists were displayed at many of the museums I visited because of their influence on American art. It was interesting to learn how their work moved art forward, including into more meditative realms as in Rothko's case.

Across the street from the MOCA was a museum called The Broad, which opened around September 2015. I first visited during November 2015. The building is an exceptional work of architecture. However, it sits across the street from the Walt Disney Concert Hall, so it's in a tough place to compete in terms of beauty. Contemporary art was also the focus of this museum, and it included pieces by great American artists like Andy Warhol. Viewing Warhol works and their descriptions provided greater insight into why historical context is important to appreciate art, which at times may not seem very artistic to the novice museum-goer. Works of art at The Broad continued to open my eyes about racial issues, especially about African-American concerns. This was important since I did not have much exposure to these issues in high school and college.

I first visited the Los Angeles County Museum of Art (LACMA) during December 2015. This museum is huge and is more crowded than the others. Due to the sheer volume of art I spent six hours at LACMA that first visit, which is much longer than the two or at most three hours that it now takes me before I reach museum fatigue. This institution features famous works of art, plenty of Picassos, a whole section on Egyptian art and mummies, a room full of Asian sculptures, even a seperate building for Japanese art. There was a memorable tiny statuette of an octopus sexually pleasuring a woman, which was interesting since I knew about the famous work of art called “Dream of a Fisherman’s Wife” and the "Tentacle Erotica" of Japan.

LACMA was busier than other museums because it was so big and so central to most of west LA. This museum also had one major feature to draw in crowds. These displays I like to refer to as "selfie stations" - notable structures or landmarks that become extremely popular places to take photos due to growing use of social media, and everyone now having a camera on their smartphone. LACMA’s "selfie station" is called Urban Light. By no means am I attempting to discredit the brilliance of this work of art, which consists of nearly two hundred street lamps of several different styles and most of which were in real use around LA during the 1920s and 30s. However, I got the impression that because you can walk through this work of art and because it is extremely "photogenic" that perhaps some of the history and meaning is lost on most of the folks taking selfies with the artwork. I felt that seeing classic movies set in LA and wandering around various neighborhoods due to my car-free lifestyle, I noticed objects like unusual street lamps in their natural element, which allowed for a greater sense of appreciation of this piece. But at least people are coming to museums and some may start their lifelong personal journey with art here.

Another museum I visited during December 2015 was The Geffen Contemporary at MOCA in Little Tokyo. I must admit that I left this institution a bit bewildered. Perhaps I found the exhibits too avant-garde for me to grasp. But failures are part of growth. I eventually realized that the more I learned about various fields of the humanities, the more context I would have to appreciate even abstract pieces of art.

In January 2016 I visited the California African American Museum in Exposition Park near the University of Southern California. There were many styles of art here that I had not seen much of in other museums. One of the most memorable works of art incorporated pieces of burnt down building from the Rodney King riots of 1992 to give the art a three dimensional space. The description discussed the importance of the riots to the African American community in LA and beyond. It also mentioned that a large group of racist LAPD cops saw that LA was progressing toward greater acceptance so they moved to Coeur d'Alene, Idaho to be around like minded people. It was novel to see an artist incorporate physical relics of a major historical event into their artwork.

On another weekend in January 2016 I had one of the most profound insights that I experienced in a museum. I visited the Norton Simon Museum in Pasadena. The layout of the museum was perfect for my studies of art. Rooms appeared organized in chronological order roughly by century. This allowed the observer to see the evolution of human thought; as if traveling through time. Religious works painted in conservative fashion were presented first. Then works depicting non-religious figures, most of whom appeared to be nobility. Paintings of these elite became less conservative; different styles and personality began to shine through. Eventually paintings depicted nature, landscapes, and still-life of food (much like how so many people take photos of their food in modern times).

These artworks continue becoming less conservative and begin to show progressive attitudes. In some ways it seems that the mental condition of the artist begins to surface. For example, Van Gogh and Monet had tough times with mental health at certain points in their lives. Perhaps this is partly a result of thinking less about deities that control your destiny and humans trying to make more sense of life without religion. It appeared that during these times there was also an increase in drugs and alcohol influencing art. As humans evolved beyond religion we began to express more feeling, emotion, mood, personality, and critical thought. Painters seemed to become more visceral. It was okay if your landscape portrait was blurry because you were experiencing a fog of depression and it was a reflection of your worldview. Moving beyond religion allowed artists to move past what the church previously deemed appropriate. This allowed painters to experiment with new styles and methods. Some painters used art as a means to tap into the subconsciousness. These changes made art more dynamic. The pace of change became quicker. As art became more progressive it began to capture the artist's philosophy and existentialism, such as in Cubism. In present times, art incorporates scientific and technological advancements, such as optical illusions and experimentation with light and space. Ultimately, I began to feel that art was depicting how the artist interprets their world. I noticed art was very psychological.

As I walked through the rooms in chronological order, I noticed that 500 years ago art was depicting elegantly decorated religious figures. Then in modern times artists painted nude lovers and prostitutes. I was overjoyed by a feeling that humans have come so far but there are ideas that seem impossible for society to accept in the present day that will be norms within a hundred years. Fine art appeared similar to jazz. Some elements of the avant garde slowly became more accepted. When you see the progress of several centuries in chronological order you witness artists breaking with tradition and ditching socially imposed structures of the mind in favor of abstract, spiritual, or other novel directions. Experiencing the radical change of art history by this museum's layout was insightful. At Norton Simon I truly felt like I made a breakthrough in my self-education of fine art. I gained the insight that over several hundred years, art served as a means of devotion, then art replicated an experience, then art became the experience in and of itself, and finally art provided a medium to experience your own mind. Artists were looking to the heavens, then at the mountains, then to new technologies, and finally within themselves.

During January 2016 we went to the LA Art Show at the convention center. This was a more practical way of experiencing art because this giant convention hall bigger than most museums in the country was filled with artists who were trying to earn a living with their passion by selling their works. Many of the pieces here were unlike most art one finds at a museum, which made attendance to this event another means of opening my mind to various elements of the art world.

While I was at Norton Simon I loved the beautiful art painted by Diego Rivera. Based on that experience, in February 2016 I took the subway to the Museum of Latin American Art in Long Beach. Two stops into the metro ride, a Latino male made a comment about African Americans while sitting next to a black male. The African American guy stood up and took off his sweater and shirt. He was ripped. He was about to beat the hell out of this racist Latino. Other African Americans on the public transport calmed him down by telling him it was not worth it. The African American man eventually told the other riders from his race that he recently graduated from a technical school and was coming from a job interview. This was a reminder of the ongoing racial tensions in LA and beyond. When I got to the museum I saw a powerful work of two black women looking into mirrors with a bottle of bleach next to them. The piece was about how lighter skin people of any race have more privilege.

Also in February 2016 I took a short subway ride to Thai Town and walked over to Barnsdall Art Park, which is home to the Los Angeles Municipal Art Gallery. This gallery was small but interesting because it featured paintings and sculptures created by LA County high school students. I was baffled by how good some of the works were, considering they were created by teenagers. It was inspirational to see the works of high school students pursuing their creative passions.

Another institute I visited during February 2016 was the Hammer Museum, which is affiliated with UCLA and near the campus. The sizable exhibition on Black Mountain College provided a great lesson about this institution's significance in shaping the American art scene around the middle of the 20th century. This college was like a commune that fostered the avant-garde. It was interesting to learn about the impact of limited structure and hierarchy on an institute of higher learning. Insights gained from this exhibition provided further context that allowed for greater appreciation of famous American artists such as Cy Twombly, whose works can be seen at many prestigious museums. Furthermore, the location of this historic college's brief existence gave me a better understanding about the artistic roots of nearby Asheville, North Carolina, which is presently one of the hippest small towns in America.

I came to the Latin American museum in Long Beach a second time in April 2016. This visit was to take a Hispanic woman here on a date. I hoped she would enjoy experiencing art from her ethnic background. At the least, I wanted to eat their house made tortilla chips again since they were so puffy, tasty, and unlike any other chip I tried in the LA area. There was a picture of Ernest Hemingway and Fidel Castro from 1960 that I enjoyed very much since Hemingway was one of the first American authors I started reading for pleasure, and because I was born in an area that was Communist. It seemed like many works of art had a common theme - how Latin America and its people were taken advantage of by the US. More lessons in art as a medium for political purposes and expression of sentiment against some governments and corporations.

A friend I met at a hostel in Bucharest, Romania then hung out with in Chisinau, Moldova was visiting LA and reached out to me. He was near Santa Monica. Since I was impressed by The Getty museum I wanted to visit the Getty Villa in Malibu. We met in May 2016 and explored the museum together. The Getty Villa is much smaller than The Getty and is more focused on Greek and Roman art and cultural artifacts. While I enjoyed this visit, it left me with regret that I was too busy trying to be cool and fooling around in middle school and high school, never paying attention to mythology. This place was a gold mine for mythology buffs. Regardless of background knowledge and context, there is plenty to see and learn at this budget-friendly LA gem.

During July 2016 I went to the UCLA campus for the first time to see the Franklin D Murphy Sculpture Garden. A nice place to enjoy art without spending a dime. I noticed a sculpture by Ukrainian-born American, Alexander Archipenko. I was happy to see an American from my motherland become a respected Cubist artist. I continued wandering around the university until I reached the Fowler Museum. One of the exhibitions was on Austronesian cultures. It was cool to see how these seafaring people traveled so far and the cultural impact they left on the places they settled. There were elaborate historic tools made out of sticks and beads that were used for navigation. What surprised me was that Madagascar was first settled by Austronesians from modern day Indonesia. Madagascar is about 200 miles off the coast of Africa yet several thousand miles from Indonesia. I learned that the language, agriculture, and culture is more similar to indigenous communities of Indonesia and Malaysia than of any country on the African mainland. Perhaps my love for swimming and bodies of water made me envious of the life of sea wanderers living on the ocean, studying patterns of migratory birds and stars to continue their journeys of thousands of miles by small canoe.

Even though I traveled to numerous countries over the previous few years, I hardly went to any museums on my travels. Now that I was learning to value such institutions, I began to incorporate museum visits on my travels. During August 2016 I visited a friend in Cleveland. Despite attending college about an hour south of Cleveland for four years I never considered going to the Rock and Roll Hall of Fame. Most of my college career, I was hanging out with international students and listening to electronica music by Europeans. I did not have a culturally American experience during those quintessentially "best years of my life." But these days I was learning to love America and its culture and art. So on this brief trip to Cleveland I visited the Rock and Roll Hall of Fame and was able to enjoy the many relics of American music culture, such as dresses worn by The Supremes. I learned to appreciate that music group on my road trips to national parks after moving to LA. At this Cleveland institution I found cool historical items like neon green and pink electric guitars from ZZ Top, and a three wheel custom motorcycle that belonged to Elvis. As an immigrant raised by parents who believed that culture only existed in the Old Continent, I would have likely never been able to understand the value of this music museum had it not been for my own desire to learn to love America.

I have never been one to make a habit of watching the same movie twice and I am unsure I have ever read the same book twice. But my experience at the Norton Simon left a lasting impression. So I went back during January 2017. People who read a book more than once tell me you always notice new observations the second time. Since my first trip to Norton Simon was as valuable as reading an art history book I wondered if this living and breathing book equivalent could offer new insights during a second visit. I still loved the thick brush strokes of Vincent van Gogh. The massive 1894 painting *Autumn: The Chestnut Gatherers* by Georges Lacombe was still my favorite because I loved the deep burning red color and wished I could be one of those people foraging in the forest. During this second visit a new piece of art spoke to me - *Leaf in the Wind* by Agnes Martin created in 1963. Around this time I was becoming obsessed with Santa Fe because of the art culture, rich history, and the mythical natural landscapes. So when I read that the artist's connection with nature led her to New Mexico I took extra time to contemplate this piece. This may have been the first time I began to appreciate minimalist art. Agnes Martin's work reinforced my growing belief that an experience can be profound and fulfilling even if minimalist - like my lifestyle. By simplifying a piece, the artist encouraged the viewer to look within rather than observing a painting of the outside world or the artist's interpretation of it. It was good to read a book a second time thoroughly rather than zipping through highlights left from the first read.

During May 2017 I wanted to visit LACMA one more time before leaving LA. I was glad to visit a second time because I got to see more works by Ukrainian-born American Alexander Archipenko. His avant-garde three-dimensional canvas art and sculpture were awe-inspiring.

As I made my way around the LA art museums I noticed one common theme shared by all of the museums except for LACMA: In an area with 10 million people, there was a lack of crowds. I wondered why so few people visited such institutions that offered so much at little cost. Perhaps Angelenos were busy in traffic, "running errands," or watching TV. Why am I judging people anyway. Less people at museums makes it more enjoyable to observe the art pieces in peace.

Learning about art allowed me to grow as a person and strengthened my appreciation for America. I was fascinated to learn about artists who were lovers of the sea, born in my birth country, and moved to New Mexico for nature. Art speaks to different people in different ways.

Everyone has unique backgrounds, world views, and interests which allow them to have their own special journey at museums. Art will speak to the same person in different ways as they evolve. There may have been paintings that I breezed by without much thought that could be so moving as to alter the course of someone's life. Learning about art opened my world to the psyche of my fellow man. Ultimately, the patron of the arts expands their worldview by growing their appreciation of the humanities.

Chapter 27: Miscellaneous Museums - The Study Of Human Progress Continued

Adventures around LA strengthened my belief in the importance of historical context to appreciate cinema, music, architecture, and fine art. I started to visit historical museums. During January 2016 we went to the Natural History Museum of Los Angeles. I was a big fan of Egyptian history since fifth grade when we mummified a store-bought chicken and buried it in the school yard as part of a class project. It surprised me to learn that Egyptians were not the only civilization to mummify. As I learned at this museum, mummification happened in Ancient Peru about 2,000 years before occuring in Egypt. They failed to teach this in grade school; another reason to pursue knowledge on your own rather than solely relying on our institutions.

During March 2016 I went to the Japanese American National Museum. My visit coincided with an exhibit about

Manzanar - a concentration camp for Japanese-Americans during World War II, which was located near Death Valley. The history of concentration camps in America is one that the country seems to prefer forgetting. Included in the exhibit was a mock concentration camp building. Vivid black and white pictures of the various living quarters and food gardens in the camp were taken by famous photographer and environmental conservationist Ansel Adams. The images included visuals of towering Sierra Nevada mountains covered with snow in the background, which conveyed the harsh environment at this infamous internment center.

During April 2016 we drove to Simi Valley, CA about an hour outside of DTLA to visit the Ronald Reagan Presidential Library. I am not a big fan of politics but I did hear good reviews about this library which is more of a massive museum. Reagan's presidential plane was inside the dining area. Visitors can tour the inside of the plane and presidential helicopter. It was spectacular to wander inside of an American president's plane. The museum also included a life-size replica of Reagan's Oval Office at the White House. One striking piece of art on the outdoor deck was a piece of the Berlin Wall that was about ten feet tall. Our visit provided a great way to spend a few hours learning about the history of America during the 1980s. On the drive home we made a rest stop in the San Fernando Valley, where I noticed a fire station with a steel piece of the World Trade Center about three feet tall and three feet wide displayed as a memorial in front. I was left feeling emotional about my adopted country that day.

During May 2016 we visited the Petersen Automotive Museum. Since LA is known for traffic and smog from cars, I figured I should learn more about car culture. I am unsure if this was a history museum or an art museum. Visiting many art museums and growing my appreciation for various forms of art, allowed me to see the well preserved automobiles as works of artistic design rather than simply relics. The cars were fantastic, especially those that were nearly one hundred years old yet shiny like new. One could appreciate the manpower that went into crafting these works of art around the time of the Roaring 20s; before the days of heavy automation in the automobile industry. There were many cars from numerous decades. It was interesting to see the design change from boxy carriage shapes to more curvy designs where frames were characterized by sleek teardrop shapes around the wheels. This major change around the late 1920s was a result of aerodynamics and the major technological innovation of using the wind tunnel for automobile design. The late 1920s and early 1930s were a grand time for car design as well as architecture built around LA. It was thrilling to see these cars in the real world then see them in classic films and vice versa. A growing appreciation of one field of the arts can bring greater fondness for other realms of artistic endeavor.

The Petersen also housed fun cars like The Batmobile. There were even automobiles that were meant to be innovative but whose trend never followed, such as full size cars with two wheels in back but only one in front. The highlight was noticing that I was appreciating art in ways I would not have expected. As I evolved, I became grateful to find beauty in the design of a building or a car.

More budget-friendly dates to historical museums and relics continued with a couple trips to Long Beach. During June 2016 we visited the USS Iowa. It was an experience like no other to wander around a massive Navy warship. We came back to the area during October 2016 to see The Queen Mary cruise ship that was active for about thirty years starting in the mid 1930s. It was cool to go back in time and see how people lived abroad cruise ships from this time. My interest in architecture and design allowed me to appreciate the artistic patterns and designs of the interior. It was a joy to experience this living and breathing piece of history that was about a thousand feet long.

During June 2016 I visited the Southwest Museum of the American Indian. It was important to learn about the people who lived in modern day America before settlers arrived. I was glad to see Southwest art and pottery with its simple yet elegant designs. Each piece seemed to receive individualized love and care as opposed to mass production by machines in low labor-cost countries. There was an affinity toward the natural world in the art and designs of the Southwest that I enjoyed. One of the most unusual bits of knowledge I gained from this museum was learning about "two-spirit" people - men who dressed and took on roles as if they were women. This term meant that this person could see the world from the perspective of both genders. Some two-spirit people who were born male would engage in pottery making whereas that role was traditionally filled by women. Two-spirit people were sometimes religious leaders. It was interesting to learn about the positive attributes that some of the native societies placed on such people nearly one hundred and fifty years ago, whereas many folks in the present are unable to accept transgender people.

A few months after my visit to the Southwest Museum of the American Indian, I went to its larger affiliate, The Autry Museum of the American West, during August 2016. My enjoyment of Native American and American West art continued here. The paintings of pristine landscapes were exceptional and motivated me to continue exploring the outdoors. I loved seeing beautiful paintings of Native Americans being one with the natural world, especially because I was coming to terms with my need for nature as a source of healing from the stress of the modern world and urban living. There were also relics like furniture from the Manifest Destiny era. One notable example was a fancy chair where the backrest was shaped like a buffalo head with horns and the front legs of the chair resembled buffalo legs. I never heard anyone in LA talk about this museum but I found it to be a not-so-hidden gem.

Chapter 28: LA's Three Judaism Museums

Although raised by Eastern Orthodox Christian parents I was more spiritual than religious. Nonetheless, I enjoyed learning about different faiths. I noticed that LA was home to three major museums affiliated with Judaism.

During July 2016 we went to the Museum of Tolerance. This institution is not solely about Jewish issues since visitors learn about discrimination and the role of negative stereotypes against other groups. The most profound experience was walking through a mock Nazi concentration camp.This model concentration camp took up about one floor. During your passage you learn about the conditions of these quarters and the people forced to endure them. Actual historic items from concentration camps such as the clothes worn by the victims as well as the whips used to beat them were on display. The dramatic experience provoked deep emotion.

In September 2016 I visited the Los Angeles Museum of the Holocaust. This museum displayed historical Jewish items such as Torah scrolls and circumcision sets from the 19th century. Nazi flags and propaganda were exhibited. I also attended a Holocaust Survivor talk for the first time. It was interesting to learn more about the Holocaust than what we were taught in school.

The third Judaism related institution I visited was the Skirball Cultural Center. This museum aims to preserve Jewish heritage and is also an education and community center. I was glad that I came here during October 2016 because one of the exhibitions was "Pop for the People: Roy Lichtenstein in L.A." This artist profile was a pleasant way to learn about contemporary American art and the innovations that were happening in the art world during the last century. It was a great way to gain a deeper understanding about one influential artist of this time.

The Lichtenstein exhibition displayed a collection of six works that started with an image of a cow which gradually became more abstract to the point that the last piece looked nothing like an animal. Titled *Bull Profile* (1973) this was a fun and informative example of one artist's perception of abstract art. The most fun part of this exhibition was to be able to enter a three dimensional life-size bedroom, which the museum made to represent the painting that Roy did in 1992 titled *Bedroom at Arles.* This painting was his modern take on Vincent van Gogh's *The Bedroom* from 1889. Coincidentally, I saw the actual van Gogh's *The Bedroom* at the Norton Simon during January 2017. The bedroom that the museum created after Roy's painting was like being in an actual comic book. It was fun and funny art that came to life. I could sit on the chairs and the bed in a room that looked like a cartoon drawing.

The exhibition informed the patron that Roy was a fan of jazz. He enjoyed taking an idea then improvising on it, which is common in this genre of music. Visitors were advised that Roy listened to Charlie Parker, Miles Davis, and John Coltrane in his studio. LA saxophonist Kamasi Washington's album called *The Epic* (2015) was playing in the gallery. This may have been the only time I heard jazz played in a museum gallery. Nonetheless, it strengthened my beliefs that different realms of art can influence one another and that jazz can have a profound impact on people's lives.

The rest of the museum was equally fascinating. There were menorahs on display where each candle holder was a prickly pear and the menorah was a cactus. I spotted another menorah where each candle holder was a replica of the Statue of Liberty. I also learned about shofars since some were displayed. These are ancient musical instruments made out of an animal's horn.

Chapter 29: Massive Eastern Temples And Religious Architecture

I discovered opportunities to learn about other religions. About twenty miles east of my apartment was the massive monastery Hsi Lai Temple. According to the temple's website the grounds encompass fifteen acres, including over 100,000 square feet of floor space. Apparently this is the largest Buddhist temple in the US. During my visit in November 2015, I was blown away to find this giant compound in an LA suburb. It looked like structure that could only be found in Asia. There were various halls, rooms, centers, gardens, countless statues, fountains, sacred spaces lit with candles and incense, and giant bells. The beautiful architecture and spacious grounds were in such immaculate condition that being here felt unreal.

The serenity of the place inspired me to go inside a shrine. I sat down and meditated to slow my mind for a few minutes. As my mind became tranquil I reflected on recent challenges and how overactive minds can blow daily struggles out of proportion and unnecessarily complicate our lives. Despite not being a Buddhist I do believe that there are certain lessons we can learn from this faith. Meditation and mindfulness can help us avoid attaching onto negative thoughts.

During August 2016 I visited The Malibu Hindu Temple. I inadvertently found out about this temple while looking at a map to find hiking trails in the Santa Monica Mountains. After noticing the Malibu Temple, I researched it and discovered it was one of the largest Hindu temples in North America. I never visited a Hindu temple before, so I thought we could stop by to admire the architecture on the way to our hike. Before driving to the temple, we stopped by a Russian food warehouse called Pacific Coast Food in North Hollywood. We loaded up on russian salads and treats for a picnic at the beach. Half an hour later we arrived at a peaceful area in the mountains where the temple was located. By this point we were starving. We stopped in the parking lot and started to feast on fried dough filled with beef. Then I realized I was eating beef a couple dozen feet from a Hindu temple. I felt bad.

We took off our shoes at the entrance and went inside the temple. There was a room with a statue of a god. A spiritual guy in a religious robe poured water into people's hands. They put the water in their mouth and on their face. Then he got a metal cone shaped item about a foot high and went around and put it above our heads. He gave each of us a banana that was resting at the base of the divine statue. Afterwards, we went to the other temple room in the basement where there were more divine statues. Then I noticed a fire pit with burning coals. There were several jars of ghee and some spoons. I assumed you put the butter on the fire so I took a wood spoon resting on the side of the fire pit and filled it with liquid ghee then poured it on the fire. The fire grew stronger. I did not know butter was flammable.

Before this visit I possessed limited knowledge of Hinduism. My trip here was well-intentioned and my curiosity about the customs was genuine. Now I had more questions than answers. Perhaps it was time to start researching information about traditions such as the purpose of the cone over our heads, who was that guy in the robe and what was his role, and what is the significance of putting ghee on a fire (if that was, in fact, part of the custom).

I was happy that my quest for fresh air led me to this ornate structure with elaborate designs such as giant elephants throughout the building.

Returning from San Diego during February 2017, we drove past Chino Hills. From the freeway I saw a gigantic temple that looked like a figment of my imagination because of its sheer size and majestic radiance during the night. I turned around to investigate. We stumbled upon the BAPS Shri Swaminarayan Mandir Chino Hills. This Hindu temple was so elaborate that it seemed there was no flat surface on the entire structure. The building's exterior with its dozen or so dome tops was covered in marvelous patterns and statues of Hindu gods. It was like a living museum and a primer on Hinduism. The doors were some of the most ornate I have seen in my life. Folks from all backgrounds are encouraged to come learn about and appreciate the temple. We got to go inside and admire the manpower and devotion used to build this place of worship. I was grateful that I went to LACMA and Norton Simon and admired their collections of Southeast Asian art, which allowed for greater appreciation of this temple.

The Hindu temple in Chino Hills was also a cultural center with a food court where we got some Indian yogurt drinks and desserts. It was culturally enlightening to experience temples that probably rival some of the biggest ones in China, Taiwan, or India; and to enjoy them within about an hour from DTLA. This was possibly the most elaborate architecture that I experienced in the greater LA area. As an immigrant, I was filled with joy to see other groups of new Americans work hard to establish faith-based centers for their communities. America was becoming more accepting of other cultures.

I also visited two Self-Realization Fellowship temples in LA. Life in DTLA led me to realize the importance of nature to my well-being. I found myself seeking any form of nature that was nearby. The Self-Realization Fellowship temples are a great source of natural atmosphere in the city.

I visited the Self-Realization Fellowship Lake Shrine Temple in Pacific Palisades during October 2016. The beautiful grounds feature a sizeable lake that you can spend an hour walking around. There is an old-fashioned windmill building, a houseboat, waterfalls with statues of divine beings and signs with quotes from the *Bhagavad Gita* holy book, and a Mahatma Gandhi World Peace Memorial. I felt a sense of peace from this spiritual center because it was surrounded by various plants and trees, and was nestled near hills. I enjoyed my time here because it was peaceful - except for the occasional Harley Davidson above the tree lined hills. A great sanctuary located a few dollars away from Santa Monica via Uber.

During December 2016 we went to the Self-Realization Fellowship world headquarters in the Mount Washington neighborhood a few miles north of DTLA. This place did not have a lake or as much acreage as the Lake Shrine location. Nonetheless, there was an abundance of trees and plants. My date and I enjoyed our walk around the well landscaped grounds. We then went inside the headquarters building where we learned about the founder and the history of the fellowship.

Another experience with religious architectural beauty occurred during July 2016. I was hoping to find a local hike so I took an Uber to Elysian Park near Dodgers Stadium. As I walked the trail along the edge of the large park I noticed some shiny gold domes reflecting the summer sun. As I approached closer, the domes appeared onion-shaped. Then I recognized a church like those in my motherland. Adjacent to the church was a tree with a swing hanging from one of the branches. I swung in the shade for a while. This Ukrainian-Orthodox church with about a half dozen gold onion-domes was beautiful. The simple yet elegant design made it appear as if it was in an Eastern

European village, not in the downtown of America's second largest city. I felt joy that another quest for hiking trails led to more divinely inspired architecture.

Chapter 30: Tulip Mania And The Affordable Experiences At The Botanical Gardens

I had wonderful experiences at museums, but I also needed time in nature. During December 2015 I visited the Huntington Botanical Gardens. This massive compound features plants from around the world, sizeable museums, and a large collection of statues. Plants are divided into gardens by category such as Palm Garden, Desert, Jungle, Subtropical, Australian, Rose, Herb, Chinese, and Japanese. The collection of cacti was impressive because there must have been hundreds of varieties, including countless shapes, sizes, and colors. The Chinese Garden with its traditional architecture and calm bodies of water looked like a film set. Peacefulness could also be found in the Japanese Garden with its bonsai shaping area and Japanese rock zen garden, with its mediative patterns raked into the gravel of this lengthy area about a hundred feet long and twenty feet wide. A curvy bridge over a pond and varying topography made the Japanese Garden look like a movie set as well.

While in the area of the Japanese Garden with numerous bonsais I noticed a dude trimming a bonsai while wearing an apron. Part of me was curious what life was like for this guy. He appeared my age. Perhaps a part of me envied his vocational pursuit. There were two dark green foldable metal chairs in front of him. The bonsai was no taller than about three feet. I should have stayed and watched him trim. Maybe I could have entered into a meditative state from mindfully observing him engage in the art of shaping a bonsai.

The gardens reminded me of the Royal Botanic Gardens in Sydney. Architecture of the museums brought back memories of the Schonbrunn Palace in Vienna. It was an 80 degree day that winter day so the experience had a Southern California touch. The second greatest benefit about the place was the respite from urban living. The scents were the best part of my experience here. I still have pleasant memories of the eucalyptus aromas in the Australian Garden. According to this institution's website, more than one hundred varieties of eucalyptus grow in the garden. Another treat to the olfactory senses is the Rose Garden where one could spend an hour smelling the seemingly infinite varieties - each with its own subtle aroma. When you live in DTLA and constantly walk past places where people have urinated, one becomes grateful for living beings that smell nice. The Huntington Gardens were bountiful for the nose, eyes, ears, and hands. The gardens were so large that despite spending five hours there, I only experienced the highlights. This is truly an exceptional place to learn about the art that the divine created in its studio.

In February 2016 we went to the Los Angeles County Arboretum and Botanic Gardens. The highlight was seeing peacocks roaming around. You can get within a couple feet from these majestic birds to admire their beauty. There was also a waterfall near some trees that provided shade, which served as our rest stop to escape the winter heat.

My tour of LA's three main gardens continued when I visited the Descanso Gardens during March 2016. The highlight was the tulips. These flowers could be seen in an array of colors, and many were multi-colored. Finance nerds are fond of tulips because of their association with the Dutch tulip mania economic bubble during the 1600s. The beauty I experienced from these tulips at Descanso allowed me to gain insight about how a nation could be so mad over tulips that it led to one of the most infamous economic busts in world history. Craft beer geeks also love tulips since a lot of the Belgian artisanal ales are served in tulip shaped glassware.

I visited Descanso at an almost perfect time of year. I enjoyed the opportunity to see the wondrous designs of half purple and half white tulips, to observe tulips whose orange base turned yellow at the top and the color gradient looked like a Tequila Sunrise, and to be stunned by satin purple looking tulips that were almost black. However, March is a time for

Cherry Blossom festivals, and the one at Descanso created a line that was several blocks long. People need their photos with cherry blossoms for social media. I even saw people wearing lacy white dresses to match the cherry blossom tree in their photo. Since all the attention was on the cherry blossoms I found quiet places to seek peace, such as a little trail of tall pines that was like a tiny forest.

Each season can provide a different experience at these gardens. They are a terrific place to learn about nature and to develop an affinity for the natural world. I am grateful for one major lesson I learned after visiting these three establishments. While I loved learning about nature from these gardens that are home to plant species from all over the world, I found that to me personally, there was no other feeling like being out in the wild. Botanical gardens felt completely different than being alone in the woods away from people and experiencing nature in its primal state while being surrounded by plants that grow there by more or less natural means rather than being shipped in for academic and tourism purposes. These three gardens provided scientific knowledge about species and environments, but being deep within nature provided me with spiritual nourishment of the soul that was beyond the information taught at a botanical garden. When I went to a botanical garden I learned about nature but when I went deep into nature I learned about myself.

I did not leave these three gardens feeling spiritually recharged and with a sense of mental clarity as I do after a three hour hike into the wilderness in relative isolation without a single view of civilization. In the mountains, the plant life is not bound by a garden's physical premises and one does not spend an afternoon absorbing facts about countless plants. Instead, out in the wild with no cell phone reception, I could enter a meditative state, slow the rapid fire thoughts of the mind, and begin to let go of mental attachments about the future or the past in favor of focusing on the present.

Nonetheless, seeing plant life held captive in an educational garden brought greater appreciation for nature in the wild. Thereafter, my strolls in the woods for the purpose of meditation, reflection, and cleansing of the soul became more abundant with the knowledge gained at educational centers. In turn, these progressive experiences allowed me to gain a better understanding of the significance that the natural world has on my wellness.

An analogy between botanical gardens and the wilderness can be found in art. There were times a few centuries ago where an artist would travel great distances to paint images of striking natural beauty or architectural marvels. Occasionally these works would find their way back to the artist's homeland so that his or her fellow citizens could see what other parts of the world looked like. Some works of art were meant to be accurate representations of a real mountain or building during a time when the majority of people would never be able to visit that place in the painting. Such works seemed like a botanical garden to me. Through it I learned about nature.

But I did not experience the real object in its natural state. Fast forward a few centuries to modern times and mindfully observe an abstract painting like those by Mark Rothko. The experience one can gain from such art can be like the meditative state one can enter by spending several hours trekking into the wild. Your experience up there in the wilderness will be uniquely yours - as it may with abstract art that encourages contemplation.

Chapter 31: The Man Smoking Marijuana From A Bong On The LA Subway Train, Traveling Around Town On A Budget, And Marine Animals Behind Glass

We went to another educational center to see nature in captivity - but instead of a garden with plants this institution displayed marine life in tanks of water. During June 2016 we visited the famous Aquarium of the Pacific in Long Beach. To avoid traffic we took the subway for one hour.

I was expecting a relatively peaceful institution where we could learn about and watch marine life. Instead, it was a madhouse. Countless sick kids were stuffed into this extremely crowded place. We only stayed for about an hour.

Then we went to dinner at Gladstone's seafood restaurant near the water. Our meal consisted of a trio of wood grilled fish including yellowtail, wahoo, and salmon. We also ate calamari.

Instead of enjoying various marine animals at the aquarium we enjoyed various marine animals at the restaurant. Then we headed back to DTLA. The subway making this route passes some of the historically most dangerous areas of LA such as Compton, Watts, and Slauson. I never saw anything out of the ordinary on the metro in greater LA except for the guy who took off his shirt when about to fight another guy. We were about halfway back to DTLA when we noticed people on the metro car moving to the next train car. I heard a lighter and noticed a guy in the corner blowing out smoke. When some of the people left to the other car he walked to the middle of the car and sat down. A bong was in his hand. His bong was about one foot high, made of blue plastic, and had two bubbles at the base. He continued to smoke marijuana while sitting down. This was happening out in the open during broad daylight. As he smoked he was coughing his lungs out. He continued smoking for about two or three metro stops. Then he got off at Compton Station. There was a family of four with two little kids near him before he started smoking. They appeared to be tourists from Europe. The mom and dad moved the family to the other train car. Their little son kept looking at the bong smoker trying to figure out what was going on. He appeared to be about eight years old and looked terrified. The woman I was with asked to move as soon as she noticed what was happening. I said he is harmless. I mentioned that a lot of people love LA for all its charm so we should appreciate this special moment. She wanted to move to another train car anyway, possibly because of the scent of burnt cannabis. She was surprised by the inconsiderate actions of this man. I was not.

I loved seeing the jellyfish and seahorses in the aquarium, but I did not feel right about it for the same reason I do not visit zoos. I have limited capacity to see animals locked up in tight quarters. I feel for the animals but also for myself. When I see animals behind glass I am reminded of myself as a mammal behind glass when I sit in an office for forty hours a week as if in some sort of human zoo built by the collective mind of society. When I make eye contact with an animal behind glass I wonder if it can sense that I feel its agony. Animals are smart after all. Society has domesticated us humans. We were wild now we are mild. I see birds fly by my office window and wonder if they look at me through the glass as I look at a marine animals in the water tank. Perhaps the birds take pity on me as I sit behind the glass while they are free like the wind. I would rather see one salamander in the wild while I am in the wilderness than to see bright fish trapped in an aquarium. It is true that some aquariums provide benefit to marine ecosystems through education and conservation, but I am unable to get over the uncomfortable feelings I get when I see animals behind glass. It is more emotional than logical. What is even more complicated is that I love to eat seafood yet I still cannot watch the sea life that I would gladly consume be trapped in small confines.

Earlier that year in January 2016 I visited another popular place with an aquarium - the California Science Center. There is a huge aquarium tank that is a tunnel for us humans to walk through. Even though you can look up and see the fish behind glass, they can also look down at you behind glass. But unlike those fish, we can escape this tunnel after a brief observation of the marine life. There is also a Touch Tank where you can touch starfish and sea urchins. But again, I much prefer to see nature in the wild than confined. However, there was one awesome feature at the California Science Center - the Endeavour Space shuttle. While standing underneath the spaceship, a foreign-born new American can marvel at this country's achievements.

Chapter 32: Expensive Experiences That I Did Not Pay For Which Further Reinforced My Affinity Towards Minimalism

During my two years in LA I had some lavish experiences. They reinforced my belief that it made little sense to spend the majority of my time pursuing the ability to afford luxuries.

On occasion, my employer had leftover box seat tickets to events at the Staples Center. The private suites facing the center of the arena were furnished with couches, tables, a big screen TV broadcasting the game you are watching, and a little kitchenette inside. Great place for schmoozing clients and networking. But sometimes no clients were in town. Leftover tickets were raffled to employees. On two occasions during January 2016 I was able to experience this luxury without paying. The first was for a basketball game to see the LA Clippers.

The second event was a boxing match. At this event I went to the end of the private suite and leaned over the edge. I could feel the collective energy of several thousand people shouting and jumping in this 20,000 person capacity venue. It was like being engulfed in a vibrating heat wave. The last sixty seconds of the match was like a fight to the death. The boxers were hitting each other at super speeds. The crowd grew even louder. I never felt this amount of concentrated and radiating human energy with my senses before. The experience generated by the excitement of the spectators was more intense than the fight.

Another high society experience I had during those two years was front of the line passes at Universal Studios Hollywood. The person who treated me to my first visit to Universal Studios acquired these front of line passes. I felt guilty at first because I assumed only fancy people could have such experiences.

I was glad to go to Universal Studios because there were some pretty cool attractions. As a kid, one of my favorite movies was the 1995 film *Waterworld* with Kevin Costner. I was grateful to experience the Waterworld show with people driving boats, people jumping all around the huge stage, and pyrotechnics. In addition, since I love *The Simpsons* and it is an icon of American culture, it was fun to visit the Simpsons town, go inside Moe's bar, eat a burger at Krusty Burger, and eat a giant pink and sprinkled Simpsons donut that was bigger than my head. That donut was the size of a small pizza. My date and I could not finish it.

The Harry Potter village was still open at this time. I never read or saw Harry Potter books or movies but it was nice to try Butterbeer, which tastes like cream soda that was around twenty years ago when I was a kid. The Harry Potter ride was entertaining as well. At this point in my life I was ultra lean so eating a portion of a massive donut and drinking a cup of extremely sweet carbonated syrup left me with a spike and a big crash. Perhaps the junk food temptations at such places are a reason I prefer to stay away. All that sugar caused me to perceive the hoards of people as greatly irritating. Luckily we got to sit for a while after our sugar crash as we rode the tram around the movie sets for *Jaws*, Hitchcock's *Psycho*, and other films. That was a fun and informative way to avoid crowds for a while.

During February 2016 a date got us tickets for good seats to see a magic show at the Pantages Theater in Hollywood. This is another classic theater built around the 1930s like some of the movie palaces in downtown. This large theater has a seating capacity of nearly 3,000. This was my first time at a magic show. Perhaps I did not have much context to appreciate the intricacies of magic, but I was impressed by the architecture and design of the theater.

Ultimately, I was happy to experience Universal Studios without spending my own hundred bucks because I doubt I would have come otherwise since I prefer to avoid fair like settings with junk food. I echo that sentiment with regards to box seats for sporting events as well as the good seats at the fancy magic show. These experiences strengthened my commitment to avoid slaving away to make a little more money so I can become accustomed to private suites, front of the line passes, and excellent seats at places and events where I do not even want regular seats or regular line passes. I was grateful for those experiences, especially because they seemed like such typical LA activities, but these fancy activities were not ones I needed to take part in again. It was nice to be growing up and becoming comfortable with my own values.

Chapter 33: Relaxing In A Korean Sauna That Looked And Felt Like A Pizza Oven And How Most Of The Coolest Experiences Were Extremely Cheap

I loved going on adventures that are budget-friendly and finding unusual experiences that cost very little. Some amusing adventures cost zero dollars. One free LA experience is a visit to The Last Bookstore. This purveyor of novels is the most quirky bookstore I have visited. Conveniently located in DTLA, I did not even need to pay for a train ticket or an Uber. I first visited this local gem during November 2015. There is a circular tunnel about ten feet high against a wall which is made of hundreds of used books. There is a large walk-in vault that houses horror books. There are fun little works of art like a typewriter on a desk with a long scroll of paper coming out and reaching the ceiling. Some books were positioned to look like birds flapping up toward the roof while other books were on the ceiling. The two story establishment has plenty of comfy couches where one can enjoy flipping through novels.

Another free institution in LA is the Annenberg Space for Photography. This cultural institution was so stellar that I was shocked by the free admission. We first came here during July 2016 when they were featuring an exhibit on refugees. There was a powerful contemporary photo of a boy carrying food for Ukrainian refugees in a camp on the Russian side of the border conflict. This image spoke to me because there was an ongoing armed conflict on the border of Ukraine and Russia and no one seemed to care - not even when Russia took the huge landmass that is Crimea from Ukraine. It seemed like the largest land grab in recent times went unpunished by any government. Furthermore, as someone who left Ukraine and lost the citizenship of my birth country in order to leave, I experienced strong emotions from the photo.

The free tour of LA continued with a brief visit to a place that not many Angelenos know exists - The Piñata District in DTLA. People come here for their pinata needs. There are all kinds of other goodies like fireworks for the Fourth of July and New Years, dried chilies and spices, candies to stuff into piñatas, and people cooking corn on a grill on the sidewalk in case you get hungry from trying to decide which pinata among the hundreds available you want. The Piñata District is also a few blocks from Santee Alley - a long narrow alley that serves as an open air clothing market. The clothes and accessories looked cheap. The crowds were perhaps the thickest of any place in LA - even worse than Hollywood where the stars are on the ground or the Santa Monica boardwalk on a summer day.

During those years in LA I first heard of "Blue Zones" - five regions in the world where people have the longest lifespans. I enjoyed learning about the similarities shared by these small communities across four continents. These zones appear to provide evidence about the importance that sense of community and purpose seem to have on longevity when combined with a healthy mostly plant based diet and moderate daily exercise. Only one of these zones is in the US and it is found in Loma Linda, California. Loma Linda has a large community of Seventh Day Adventists whose lifestyles help increase lifespans. I was astounded that a community with the longest lifespan in America lives only sixty miles east of the most polluted major metro area in the US - LA.

We drove to Loma Linda during March 2016 to see how these folks live. Since they do not drink, there was not much of a bar scene. We stopped by one of the grocery stores in the center of this community. I spotted the largest selection of vegetarian products that resemble meat I have ever seen. Some of these include canned vegetarian breakfast sausages and no-meat bacon bits sold by weight in the bulk goods section. While driving around the quaint town and pleasant residential areas we did not notice any extravagant homes or ultra fancy cars. The city is near a hiking trail so we took a stroll through nature.

We also stopped by a cute town nearby called Redlands to visit an artisanal bean-to-bar chocolate maker, Parliament Chocolate. Surprisingly, LA did not have many artisan chocolate makers or even craft breweries within the county limits before 2015. Our trip to Loma Linda served as a reminder that one does not need much to have health and life satisfaction. It is possible that if one wishes to live long they might want to place more emphasis on social support systems and finding some degree of meaning in their life rather than dedicating most of their time to selfish pursuits.

My little sister visited during August 2016, so I took it up a notch and spent a few dollars on an activity. The US Bank tower was on its way to losing its title as the tallest building in LA. To attract attention they made an enclosed see-through slide on the outside of the building called Skyspace. You slide from one of the top floors to the one below while about a thousand feet above ground. It was a tacky way to spend about ten bucks for about ten seconds of fun. While we were up there we enjoyed the views of sprawl and smog.

My sweet spot for weekend entertainment was about twenty to twenty five dollars for a museum or a show. Within this range I could go out one night a week, experience joy, and learn - all without having to stray from my financial plan. Around this price range I visited a comedy club for the first time in my life. We went to the Laugh Factory in Hollywood during December 2016. It was hilarious. Definitely worth the money to spend a couple hours on this type of fun. In addition, abstaining from alcohol for financial goals encouraged me to order a couple glasses of tea instead of two pricey alcoholic drinks to meet the two item purchase requirement.

Another supremely worth the money experience in the twenty five dollar range was visiting Wi Spa in Koreatown. Sights, smells, and the noises of the city are almost non-existent inside so you can relax and escape from the feeling of being in the core of a major urban area.

I visited this jjimjilbang Korean bath house during November 2015. In fact, I believe this was my first time visiting any spa or bath house in the US. This 24 hour spa is a huge four story complex. Basement is women only. First floor is men only. Second floor is common area.

I took a shower, dipped into a jacuzzi, laid on a hot stone floor, then went into a steam room. Afterwards, I walked past the room full of leather reclining chairs and found the "sleeping room" where I took a nap on a leather sleeping pad with legs, which I could not really call a bed per se. After my nap I went into the common area with traditional Korean saunas. One is basically a large fridge set to 41 degrees F. Then there is a “salt room” where you lay on pink stones of some sort, which is 120 degrees F. The jade room with jade rocks stuck to the walls and ceiling is about 120 degrees F, and apparently the jade has some mineral healing properties. Perhaps the funniest looking room is the one shaped like a stone dome, and at 201 degrees F, it looks and feels like being in a pizza oven. Then I entered the "clay room" where the floor is covered a foot deep with brown clay balls the size of marbles. You lay on balls and sweat. And all the sweat from you and the previous person to lay there runs down onto the balls. You find that you are covered by sweaty balls.

After relaxing in the saunas I decided to get a massage, which is extremely rare for a frugal person. However, massages are probably necessary for someone who spends the bulk of their waking life sitting at a desk. The "accupressure" massage cost $60, but if you buy one they drop your $25 entrance fee to the spa to $15 so the whole package is $75. Half hour of the massage was by hand. Then the masseuse did about 20 minutes of the massage with her feet, which explains why the sheet was still on my back during the therapy. Now I see why it only costs $60 instead of a $100. She was walking all over me with her feet. I finally looked back and noticed there was a pole near the ceiling that she held onto. By this means, there was pressure, but not so much that you would get hurt. It seemed like she was a professional because at times she would even arch her feet to squeeze my body. Other times she used her toes. Occasionally she used her heels. I was impressed. The last ten minutes I laid on my back while she massaged my arms, shoulders, head, and ears. Not bad for $60. I considered this big ticket expense preventative care.

After the massage I ate at the Korean restaurant inside. The table was one where you sit on the floor to eat. This was the first time I ate in a restaurant barefoot. While waiting for the food, a Korean game show was on the TV. About a dozen contestants were each holding a roll of toilet paper. They were trying to see whose roll could go the furthest without tearing. For dinner I ate soup, bulgogi Korean beef, rice, an egg, and kimchi. All for twelve dollars. Afterwards I went to the different sauna rooms to digest. This was a great way to spend four hours.

It was nice to enjoy LA's offerings without spending on pricey events, restaurants, clothing shops, and theme parks.

Chapter 34: Most Of The World Wants To Experience Los Angeles Area Beaches - Perhaps Thanks To The Show 'Baywatch', Subway Train To The Ocean, Budget-Friendly Cycling, And LA Traffic In Bike Lanes

Many people from around the world want to visit or move to LA because of the beaches and climate. My experiences with Santa Monica and Venice Beach follow.

About one year after I moved to LA, getting to the beach became cheap. Since I did not want to pay for pricey ride shares to the beach I found other parts of LA to explore that first year. Then the city extended the Expo Line train to Santa Monica. The subway station was three blocks from the beach. This was major news to a car-free minimalist.

Santa Monica station opened May 2016. I took the light rail to the beach that opening weekend. It was super packed.

When I got off at the Santa Monica terminus there was a five piece mariachi band dressed up and playing festive music. Now I could access the beach for about two dollars. The commute was just under one hour.

In July 2016 I went to the Venice Beach Freakshow. Spending one hour at my first freakshow was possibly the best use of five dollars I ever spent in LA. While some may find such venues exploitative, none of the performers appeared that they were there against their will.

Freakshows are historically significant. There are films and literary works where such performances are referenced. I was doing due diligence to be a more well-rounded patron of the arts.

A tall man with long blonde hair fed a giant hook through his nose and out of his mouth. He also swallowed a sword. There was a psychotic looking clown that I imagined would haunt the sleep of the younger people in the crowd in the intimate venue. There was a room with a two headed turtle and two headed snake with an orange and white pattern.

After the freakshow I walked to the concrete skatepark on the shore to reminisce on my teenage years. Around this area people were spray painting mock walls on the sand. Since LA is full of graffiti it makes sense to provide public places for people to spray paint instead of on private property. Then I walked around the neighborhood in Venice that has canals, sort of like Venice, Italy but not really. There are cute little bridges over the canals near the multi-million dollar homes. I saw a hippo-shaped two seater pedal boat that a guy and a gal were powering with their legs while sipping champagne. I walked over to Mother's Beach in Marina Del Rey to determine its viability for open water swimming in a place without waves, but the water seemed disgusting.

Wandering around Venice was fun. But you see the writing on the wall when walking along Abbot Kinney Boulevard and noticing high end restaurants and pricey clothing boutiques. This is a contrast from the old hippie rollerblading with a guitar in his hands along the boardwalk or the group of five grungy dudes playing music with dated instruments on the sidewalk near the beach parking lot. Venice was changing. California was getting way too popular and way too rich for hippies to live on beach front properties. I was glad I got to experience Venice a few times before I left. Soon it may become a tech nerd paradise since some already call it "Silicon Beach." As it relates to tech firms, I was friends with a guy who worked at a massive gaming company near Santa Monica. He gave me a tour in February 2017. The huge Silicon Valley style campus had its own cafe, nap room, and beer everywhere inside. It's only a matter of time before gentrification pushes out the historic elements that made Venice Beach funky and full of weed smoke before recreational use was legalized here in 2018.

One of my most memorable moments at an LA beach occurred during January 2017. I walked to the end of Venice pier and watched surfers as I faced toward land. It was a warm day. A boy around the age of eight with a custom lowrider bicycle complete with a sidecar was cruising along in a t-shirt. The girl in the sidecar who appeared to be four years old was wearing a Dodgers jersey and eating a bag of Hot Cheetos. People were riding bikes in tank tops. As the cyclists passed and I went back to zenning out over surfers riding God's gift to mankind, I saw a big white object beyond the buildings. I tell myself: No, that cannot be. But, yes, it was. I saw a giant mountain range covered in snow. Not one peak but a whole range. And not only the tops. There must have been one or two thousand feet of elevation worth of snow from top down. It is quite rare to see snow in LA, especially from the beach. In fact, it is quite rare to see anything of any considerable distance through the LA smog. Sometimes one can barely see the DTLA skyline from the Griffith Observatory less than ten miles away. So I was shocked to see Mt. Baldy about sixty miles away. Standing above the sea, breathing in the salty air, and watching surfers ride waves as I sport a t-shirt without needing a sweater all while staring at so much snow off in the distance. This delightful sight made me understand why people make crazy statements such as "some of the best things in life are free." My heart melted as that snow stayed unmelted.

During February 2017 I discovered that Santa Monica has a gem of a public pool. A day pass costs seven dollars for the public. I swam about two miles that day. Since it was early in the morning the lap lanes were set to be Olympic distance, which is rare for most pools in large cities. It was nice to swim in an outdoor pool as opposed to my indoor one downtown. And I was in bliss to swim Olympic distance laps. It must have been a couple years since I swam Olympic lengths rather than doing about sixty flip turns per mile.

LAX airport is on the beach and adjacent to a town called El Segundo. During January 2017 we were in Venice Beach then Ubered to a brewery in El Segundo. I was shocked when we arrived in central El Segundo because I could smell and taste the jet fuel exhaust pollution. The center of El Segundo is practically right under where the jets take off. I was surprised that people could live in this area. Being frugal we Uber from El Segundo to the nearest subway station. A male rider was listening to metal music loud enough that the entire train car could hear. A woman kept making eye contact with me and her face expressed how annoyed she was by the music. Eventually I walked up to the middle aged man who happened to be wearing a security guard jacket. Politely, I asked him if he could turn it down. He asked why. I responded because I have a headache. Then I walked away and got back to my seat. He turned it down a tad. Then he turned it up even louder for the rest of the ride.

During January 2017 I first signed up for a bike share program in Santa Monica. You get an app on your phone, find a bike at a special bike station, and unlock it. The app charges you by time. I enjoyed riding along the boardwalk north past Santa Monica and south past Venice Beach. I used to cycle regularly when I lived in San Diego but I did not bike much when I lived in Austin or LA. So I was happy to be pedaling again, especially along the beach and on a path away from cars. I came back in February 2017 and rented a bike again. The app informed that I rode six miles in about an hour and the fare was $6.07. A fun and healthy way to spend a few bucks. Then in April 2017 I rented a bike again. This time I cycled around for an hour and a half. After this ride up and down the beach I vowed to never bike here again. The walk / bike path was way too crowded. Many parts of the path were a bike traffic jam. There were pedestrians crossing the bike lane without looking. I was hoping for a new way to relax and to get away from cars and traffic but this was almost worse. What should have been exercise to de-stress actually caused more stress.

Chapter 35: Feng Shui And Cosmetic Eyelid Surgery

One of my favorite hikes in LA was in the mountains near Arcadia, California. During March 2017 we went hiking there. My hiking buddy got a cut, so we went back to civilization for first aid supplies. The nearest drug store was in Arcadia. This was my first time driving around this suburban town and I noticed this city seemed very Chinese. So I started researching. Fortunately for me, my coworkers were Chinese and Taiwanese, and familiar with the Chinese population of the San Gabriel Valley.

Arcadia is essentially the Chinese Beverly Hills. I read about rich Chinese in Arcadia making their mansions feng shui friendly. Over the next several weeks my coworkers were teaching me about feng shui.

Other than wealthy Chinese, Arcadia is known for free roaming peacocks - like the ones at the Los Angeles County

Arboretum nearby. Someone familiar with Chinese culture once told me that peacocks are good feng shui because they represent the phoenix. In China, the dragon is a good sign and the phoenix is the wife of the dragon. Together they are yin and yang and create a good balance.

I was learning the intricacies of feng shui like how some Chinese do not like to live in cul de sacs because there is potential risk that bad energy cannot flow through and gets stuck there. But it is not so simple; if the cul de sac is at the top of a hill and the rest of the street is downhill then it is ok because water-like energy can flow downhill. Historically, cul de sacs where the end is at the bottom of a hill is not good because a horse might have a hard time stopping and run into your house. However, there are ways to balance the not ideal feng shui if you are stuck living at the end of a cul de sac, such as placing a fountain on your property so that the flowing water will keep the energy circulating instead of remaining stagnant.

Feng shui means "wind-water." I also learned that wind can be good because it can move your sailboat but it can be bad because it can blow your house down. Likewise, water can be good because you can drink it to sustain life, but it can also drown you. Around this time I began to notice this stuff was complicated. Aspects of feng shui seemed superstitious. Apparently, there was also a belief that feng shui principles come from the East and cannot be accurately applied in the West.

In Arcadia houses are being torn down so that mansions can be built. It appears there are professionals ready to help wealthy folks with their feng shui needs. There are a lot of elements to consider. Stairs cannot be a certain way, doors need to be another way, the house itself must be on a certain part of the block, such as in the middle instead of the corner, driveways need to be another way, and the list goes on. Some home buyers avoid buying a house if the number four was in the address. I was too minimalist to worry about all this fuss. Nonetheless, it was interesting to learn about this cultural aspect and to gain an appreciation for the level of detail considered. I loved learning about different cultures and how new Americans assimilated in a more inclusive America while maintaining their beliefs.

Around February 2017 someone from Asia told me about double eyelid compared to single eyelid. He advised that because his lineage was close to the northern border of China near Mongolia and Russia, his eyes were characterized by double eyelids, which is what most Caucasian people have. Prior to this discussion I possessed zero knowledge about different eyelids. This person then informed me that surgery from single eyelids to double is the most common cosmetic surgery in Korea. Since I was living about two miles from Koreatown, I checked a website for reviews of restaurants and other businesses, for "eyelid surgery" and set the location to Koreatown. There was a plastic surgery office with 89 reviews on Yelp that showed a rating of 4.5 out of 5 stars. This business displayed dozens of before-and-after photos of people who underwent procedures there, including numerous photos of single to double eyelid changes.

These lessons in Chinese culture allowed me to become more sensitive to other people and more detail-oriented. During May 2017 I was in Arcadia and got a meal at the famous high-end Taiwanese steam bun chain Din Tai Fung. A lot of Asian dumplings are called potstickers. I have eaten these since I was a kid via frozen packaged versions from the grocery store. But I recently learned from a Chinese colleague that potstickers actually have to stick to the pot where they develop a thin crepe-like layer, which hold the dumplings together in one unit. Learning about these subtle nuances helped me appreciate my first time eating "real" pot stickers.

Having a genuine interest in the culture of my colleagues and sharing in their customs made work enjoyable. During January 2017 I received a lucky red envelope with money inside from a coworker. The envelope pictured a cockerel on it because it was the Year of the Rooster. I thought to myself that I already had a year and a half of a rooster next door crowing every morning that I do not need another year of the rooster. Perhaps that one dollar in the lucky envelope would help expedite my departure from LA and the rooster.

In July 2016 I was feasting on dim sum with my team in Chinatown. One of the coworkers told me that was the first time they feasted on dim sum with a white person at the table; even though this person spent a large portion of their life in the US. Then I reached for some saucy pork ribs in a small bowl.

Instead of using my chopsticks which I already put in my mouth, I used a Chinese soup spoon to scoop some out and onto my plate. I was advised this action offended the entire race of Chinese people. During this meal one of the team members shared a story about a Chinese emperor from a few hundred years ago who found it sexy when women's feet were small, which led to "foot binding." As part of this ancient custom, some elite women would have their feet bound up tightly from childhood so that their feet would not grow much in length. The feet sort of grew on themselves and became kind of squished but still short in length. Apparently the emperor thought the way this made women walk was sexy. But these women could not walk much, so only elite could do this since they had servants to get stuff for them. This was an interesting custom to learn about while we were sucking the skin off chicken feet.

I even learned a little about Chinese grammar. Apparently, Chinese does not have plural. For example, in Chinese they would say "six person" not "six people." You are already saying six in front, so it is clear there is more than one. Hence there is little point of the extra step to change "person" to plural "people." Their language seemed a bit more efficient in some ways.

Some of the best meals I ate in LA were with people who provided me with some sense of community as I was exploring this Land of Asian Cuisine for two years. These folks introduced me to all kinds of novel dishes. I learned a meal is more enjoyable when you genuinely appreciate learning about the foods, customs, and culture of the people with whom you spend a large amount of your waking life. We did not need to be treated to steak and wine or pricey sushi; I was grateful for an occasional visit to a budget-friendly ethnic restaurant that came along with good cheer. And to think… a friend getting a little cut on a hike indirectly allowed me to create more cohesion with my team because the cut led to a detour, which sparked more desire to learn about the customs of my coworkers' homeland. Often times we get frustrated by life when it takes us off our planned course. I was slowly learning to be more welcoming of detours as a source of little gifts from the unpredictable journey called life.

Chapter 36: New Shoes Come With Blisters For A Couple Months - Sometimes New Challenges Do Too

Life was not simply eating new foods and going on budget-friendly adventures to learn about America. In fact, my situation in LA got off to a rocky start. The first four months were trying.

The interview for the job in LA was brief so I did not have a complete understanding of what I was getting into. All I knew was that I got an offer quickly and it was for significantly more money.

However, up to that point in my career I worked in environments where I was told what the issues were and how to address them. In addition, I worked with teammates in similar roles who I could turn to for support. When I started this new job I formed the perspective that I would not be given much detail about the issues or how to fix them. Instead I would be told to figure out the details surrounding any issues and I would then have to create solutions and implement policies. This was the first time I was thrown into an environment that appeared "sink or swim." Furthermore, there was limited guidance since this new team was being built from scratch. Being new to a figure-it-out-on-your-own work setting, I did not sense that I was empowered to succeed. I found myself in quite a pickle.

I needed to adapt to different types of personalities that I had not worked with previously. At times this challenge was stressful. After plenty of reflection, I was able to convince myself that this was a lecture from life on dealing with people. This was the first time in life I began to realize a valuable lesson: You cannot change others, you can only change what you think about them. I rationalized that some people might be dealing with issues in their personal lives that I have zero insight into, so I should try to be more empathetic towards others.

It is possible that being in such an environment for the first time made me question myself and this lack of confidence led to worry. I found myself in unfamiliar territory but I needed to find strength within to overcome this challenge. In August 2015, I tried to find the silver lining. This was the first time I genuinely tried to convince myself of the following: If I need to part ways with this job any day, this will force me to be grateful for each day and live more in the moment. However, this work challenge was too small to cement such a valuable life lesson in my mind. I did not need to believe it badly enough to completely adopt it as a core tenet of my life's philosophy till years later.

Instead of adopting a lifelong commitment to live day to day, I came up with the following rationalization. During August 2015 the leather dress shoes I wore to work got a hole in the sole. I was frugal and disliked shopping for clothing, so I would wear my shoes till they got holes. At any given time, I usually only own one pair of shoes for work, one for hiking, and one for all other activities. It was time for a new pair of work shoes. Since I rarely bought leather shoes I forgot how uncomfortable they were when new. After I got new leather shoes it took more than two months before they were worn in. For a couple months I experienced discomfort Monday through Friday. I had blisters for the months that it took these shoes to break in. But when they finally broke in, they fit like a glove. I was filled with joy when this moment finally came. It made me wonder why people want to purchase new shoes often. But, more importantly, it made me realize that sometimes a challenging situation can be like a new leather shoe - you need a couple months or so before the discomfort goes away. After my new shoes starting fitting snug they were exceptionally comfortable for about two years - till that pair got a hole. Comparing this trying situation to a shoe saved me. It provided me with the strength to keep going despite the blisters.

To be fair, it is possible that I was not accustomed to intense environments where one is expected to hit the ground running. For this reason I am glad that I overcame this challenge because I am now more comfortable jumping into such job roles.

Overall, this was a good lesson from life. Sometimes you get thrown into a situation that makes you uncomfortable. If you want to overcome the challenge then it is up to you to find the silver lining and to start seeing the glass half-full. Remember your intention for what got you into this situation in the first place. In this case, I got into this job because I wanted to pay off my college loan quickly to become debt free. Learn to endure the discomfort a bit while remaining focused on your original intention (as long as it is not killing you or causing major health issues). Lastly, focus on the present day and do the best you can during that specific day.

I am grateful that I persevered because after I left this job I was able to get another position where I was not told what the problem and solution were but rather I was told to find the problem and make my own solution, then find a way to implement that solution. Secondly, by persevering through the perceived difficulties, I ended up developing a strong relationship with one of my favorite bosses up to this point in my career. He was the kind of guy that would go to bat for his team.

Over time, his kind but firm management style and supportive attitude made me more at ease, which allowed me to become more productive. As my productivity and confidence grew I began to take on more challenging tasks. Then I completed one big project on my own and I felt like I gained his trust. Even though, like most Americans, I cannot say the work I was doing was tremendously meaningful if one were to judge it by amount of earth or lives saved, I can say that it felt wonderful to be confident in your abilities and to earn the trust and respect of your supervisor by your hard work. It was pleasing to help resolve issues if the boss was out of the office, which earned even more trust. This in turn allowed me to get even more exposure to other interesting projects and opportunities, which expanded my knowledge and skills. These positive strides in my employee-supervisor relations gave me a sense of pride. Perhaps I simply needed someone to believe in me so that I could then believe in myself. And for that empowerment I am very grateful our lives crossed paths. In the end I was able to accomplish my goals of paying off my college loan and sticking with a job for two years.

Chapter 37: LA Pollution, Nasal Polyps, Silver Lining, And The Detours In Life As Gifts Not Detours

Challenges come in various shapes and sizes. Some are small in size but are in the shape of nasal polyps. Sometimes in the midst of an uncomfortable situation it is difficult to see the silver lining and how it may lead to growth, especially when these challenges are abnormal growths. Part of growing up was learning acceptance. Time for reflection is important to derive positive lessons from a challenging situation. I needed to accept that life was not simply seeking pleasure and avoiding pain. These insights led me to develop gratitude for the little things in life. Personal growth resulting from abnormal growths is possible depending on the perspective. Developing nasal polyps from pollution brought my attention to the fact that my minimalist life in terms of material possessions and square footage was only an introductory chapter in this book called

Life. Letting go of materialism was fairly simple compared to what came next. In addition to letting go of attachments to a personal automobile, caffeine, and most modern day electronics, it was time to let go of my attachment to an unexpected product - black pepper.

About one year after I moved to DTLA, I noticed my sneezes were painful. In October 2016 I put a sticky note on my pepper shaker stating "I think black pepper causes painful sneezes." This was a reminder to temporarily avoid black pepper in attempts to isolate what was going on with my body and see if I developed an allergy. After quitting black pepper, the painful sneezes continued.

In December 2016 I formulated a new theory: People who live in extremely polluted cities will experience a biological adaptation and evolve to survive in their environment - thus they will experience rapid growth of nose hair, which will act as an air filter to block pollutants from entering their body. I wondered if men living in polluted cities went bald faster because energy to grow hair on the head was redirected to increase nose hair. Then I found a thought-provoking ninety second commercial. There are Chinese people, babies, and even dogs who have really long nose hair. There are adds in the background for nose hair products and special nose hair haircut salons. Views of a large city covered in thick smog are shown. These people in the smog choked cities are meant to represent survivors of the pollution era. The end of the commercial has the tagline: "Change Air Pollution Before It Changes You."

I went to the doctor during December 2016 and told him sneezing is painful. He asked me to blow hard on a tube. He said my lungs appear fine so he ruled out asthma. Lastly, he looked up my nose. Then he told me I have nasal polyps - bumps in the nostrils caused by environmental irritants. There was now less space for the sneeze to travel through and hence the pain. He prescribed Flonase and Zyrtec. I told him I do not take drugs and asked if there were any alternatives. He said even if I took these medications they will not change the environment. He told me many people in LA have this issue. Then he mentioned taking these meds should bring the polyps down in two months. I decided against taking these pills. The meds are a band-aid that do not change the root cause. I was for sure done with LA. Polyps themselves are not necessarily bad initially. But they can lead to complications in the long term, possibly even breathing issues that impact mental functioning.

I was surprised that I developed these symptoms in only about a year of living and working in DTLA. Between work, lunch, and gym, everyday I walked around DTLA for over one hour a day on average. During these walks I passed dozens of smokers and polluting vehicles blowing their exhaust fumes in my face.

I vowed to move to a city with clean air. It saddened me that I was trying to live an environmentally conscious lifestyle without adding to the pollution and traffic. Instead of being rewarded or at least left in peace, I felt penalized.

During December 2016 I canceled my gym membership where I swam almost daily. The more I walked around in DTLA the worse I felt. I would walk to and from work two times a day for a total of forty minutes. Walking to the gym was an additional fifty minutes round trip. I needed to cut my time outdoors in DTLA as much as possible. There was only a few months left in LA before I reached my two year mark. Instead of swimming, I started doing yoga at home a few days a week and eating less for dinner. It was strange that not going to the gym made me healthier.

In March 2017 the painful sneezing got worse and turned into migraines. This was the first time I experienced such chronic agony in my head. Living and working in filthy DTLA became a nightmare. Every time I walked to or from work and the gym I crossed a bridge over the 110 freeway made up of about ten lanes of traffic. As soon as I crossed this bridge I would walk past a building with a logo on top for a company called L.A. Care. There were always folks smoking outside. The law stipulated smoking was prohibited within fifteen feet from a building entrance. So instead, they all went to the sidewalk where I walked past them. It was ironic that a company affiliated with the health industry was indirectly creating an unhealthy environment for pedestrians. Perhaps they could have created a smoking area in the parking lot. I then passed a LA municipal building and a hotel where people smoked out front near the sidewalk.

Since my apartment was close to downtown I was surrounded by cars. And because LA County has millions of extremely poor people, there were countless old automobiles which polluted excessively. California has one of the strictest vehicle smog policies of any state but somehow many cars were getting around these laws that require automobiles to be smog checked in order to receive registration from the DMV. There are lots of people in poverty who drive without registration. California also has a classic car exemption for cars built before 1975. If you own a car manufactured before 1975 you do not need to have it smog checked. While I understand the importance of preserving history, all cars should pass smog. Classic cars and antiques can go into museums. This law is strange because the cars that pollute the most get a free pass.

Due to migraines and constant painful sneezing, I started to be on the lookout for polluters everytime I walked somewhere. Fire engines were some of the worst polluters. Their exhaust pipes were massive, the engines ran on diesel, the exhaust pipes faced sidewalks, and fire trucks were often left with their engines on and idling even if they were parked. I still have bad memories of massive black clouds of exhaust coming onto the sidewalk as parked fire engines start driving. The diesel Dodge ambulances used by the LAFD also had the exhaust pipes on the sidewalk side. It was ironic that vehicles which were meant to save lives harmed people. I hope future public vehicles move to electric.

In two years of living in DTLA I only saw one fire. Granted it was a big fire and I could see huge amounts of smoke on the other side of downtown. However, I would hear fire truck sirens a dozen times a day. Some of the calculus did not add up. I understood that firefighters are first responders so they need to rush when people have a heart attack or a drug overdose. I wondered if first responders could drive a Prius. I asked someone with firefighting experience. This person advised me that fire engines have a crew of four so they can get heavy individuals out of a tough situation, and they need their heavy equipment for extraction and forcible entry. I still believe four strong fire fighters and their equipment might be able to fit in a vehicle that is a little more compact than one of the largest polluters in the city. Of course, fire trucks were not the only big diesel polluting vehicles. Armored money delivery trucks and uniform delivery vans drive around the city all day. And the money trucks also love to leave their engines on while parked.

Even graffiti and people pissing on the sidewalks cause pollution. Some of these downtown establishments hired people who used power washers to remove graffiti from the buildings or urine from the sidewalks in front of their business. Power washers ran on generators. When walking past these generators I started sneezing and getting migraines. I wondered if there were smog related regulations for generators. Many are quite old.

After developing sensitivities to pollution I noticed strange sights when visiting suburbs. LA is dry and prone to water shortages, yet people water their lawns to grow grass and pay workers to landscape their yards with polluting lawn mowers, blowers, and other equipment. Furthermore, the landscapers drive to the site, often in old vehicles that pollute quite a bit. It seemed that it could be a win-win for homeowners and the environment if people used gravel and cactus to create a more desert-like yard.

I began to research pollution and its impact on health. LA's population was growing rapidly. Incomes were also rising, so the city needed fancy residences. New luxury apartments were built right on the freeway. I walked past one everyday. The sign out front claimed they were "elegant resort style apartments" or something along those lines. But the complex was right on the I-110 freeway with its ten lanes of traffic. People's patios were a few feet from a mega highway that was congested most of the day. I was unable to understand how people could pay expensive rents for horrible living conditions. I read that the rule of thumb for a healthy living space was to be at least 500 feet from a freeway, but preferably 1,000 feet away. These luxury buildings were popping up all over greater LA. Back in the day no one wanted to live next to a polluted freeway, but now the desire to live in LA was so strong that long term health took a back seat. Articles were written about these residences built adjacent to freeways, which they called "black lung lofts." Some were suggesting that research showed dust particles from car brakes was so fine that they could get through building air filters. When there is more traffic, there is more braking, thereby more harm to folks in the area. Some advocacy groups wanted disclosures on apartment lease agreements which would advise that children living next to freeways may experience lung development issues. It did not appear that many policy makers or developers believed this alleged science stuff.

I had little control over the environmental situation. But I did have control over my residential location. My experience with harmful pollution led me to research cities to move to with good Air Quality Index ratings. I learned a lot about cities with favorable air conditions such as Salinas, CA; Flagstaff, AZ; and Santa Fe, NM. At this point my ego did not care much about career and I figured I could find a decent job in any city with at least 50,000 people.

I became passionate about air quality and started looking for jobs in air quality compliance. During March 2017 I noticed a job titled "Air Pollution Specialist" working for the California Environmental Protection Agency's Air Resources Board. Unfortunately, the job was in Sacramento and I had zero desire to live there. But Santa Fe, NM seemed appealing. The city of about 70,000 people was also a state capital, so there were government jobs. It was considered the third largest market for art in the US after NYC and LA, since it is home to so much history related to Native Americans and The American West. The town has an elevation of 7,000 feet and there is a ski resort within twenty miles. But most importantly, there was little congestion and the air was clean up in the high desert, far from any major metropolitan area.

My fascination with some of these clean air cities grew because of attributes beyond air quality, thereby inspiring me to visit them. During February 2017, we took a road trip from LA to Sedona, Flagstaff, and Santa Fe. This was my first time experiencing the majestic qualities of the Southwest. A few days prior to starting the long drive I sought guidance by watching the culturally significant American road trip film *Easy Ride*r (1969) with Peter Fonda and Dennis Hopper.

Santa Fe and New Mexico inspired me to apply for a job there. During March 2017, I interviewed for a state job located in Santa Fe. The position was "Food Program Compliance Officer." I advised the interviewer that I spent two years on the road flying and driving around the country to conduct compliance inspections of financial advisors so this could be a good role for me since the core skill sets are similar. The job entailed driving around the entire state and visiting organizations that take public funds for food to ensure those resources are not being misused. Part of the job included visiting Native American reservations, which I thought would have been an eye-opening experience. Towards the end of the call, the interviewer asked if I had any experience with government health programs. For a fraction of a second I was close to responding that I did not have any such experience. But then I was quick on my feet and replied that as an immigrant child, my single-mother was on a public food assistance program and we benefited from this public resource so I valued these programs and wanted to ensure that people do not misuse them. It was a great conversation but ultimately it was difficult to get a job in another state when they do not have funds to fly out candidates interviewing for lower level jobs. It would have been nice to help maintain public assistance programs. While living in DTLA I went to the 7-Eleven convenience store near my apartment to buy sparkling water. While in line a young male next to me asked if he could buy my water for me with food stamps if I purchase a Black & Mild cigar for him with my money. I told him I cannot support this scheme. He got aggressive with me. So I asked him “Shouldn’t you be getting food with that?” to which he replied “But I’m good.”

Getting polyps indirectly led to insights about America. I learned about Santa Fe, the off-grid communities and artist colonies in Taos, and all kinds of interesting facts about New Mexico and the Southwest. I laughed at life. During my two years of auditing financial advisors all around America I always avoided New Mexico when it came to picking destinations for my business trips. I thought New Mexico was a wasteland. About three years later I began to love it so much that I wanted to move there. I dreamed of starting a new life where I could wear bolo ties, eat green chile, and mingle with artists while enjoying fresh mountain desert air.

Sometimes life is better at making plans for you. I would learn to accept and trust and maybe even one day embrace the "detours" from my plan that were created by life. It was important for me to learn to love the "detours" so much that one day I would not even think of them as diversions from my planned path; rather that life was much bigger than me. And even though sometimes these detours may be painful, life will be okay in the end. In fact, a life full of detours is likely much more interesting than a life where you fulfilled every plan you made. Such reflections would one day allow me to have more faith in the cosmos.

Furthermore, this experience with pollution and polyps made me realize the importance of the environment to my health. You truly do not know the value of something you take for granted everyday until it is taken away. I began to value clean air very much. This made my hikes and time in nature all the more enriching. But I did not have to get out of the urban core to start appreciating the natural world. I was so deprived of nature that I began to love the rain. I got so conditioned that rain would clean the piss off the streets and create a temporary cleansing of the air quality in DTLA that I would almost start singing in the rain like Gene Kelly. Whenever it rains in Southern California most people complain, but I would take a deeper breath to ease the pain. There was not much nature downtown so I took what I could get even if that meant getting wet.

A few days after I first found out that I was diagnosed with nasal polyps, I went to a cemetery called Forest Lawn. I explored many museums and after I visited the main ones in LA, I started going to lesser known institutions. Somehow I found out that this cemetery had a museum and that the architecture of the mausoleum was exceptional. Walking from the entrance of the cemetery to the museum then to the mausoleum was peaceful. There were hardly any cars in this massive cemetery, which provided a nice break from walking around pollution all day in DTLA. The one strange sign I noticed read "Flower theft is a crime punishable by imprisonment - Penal Code 602." I knew LA was home to hundreds of thousands of people living in poverty but it seemed depressing that people would steal flowers from graves. As I continued walking I was able to appreciate all the greenery provided by the well maintained grass and trees on the expansive hills. Perhaps I developed an appreciation for cemeteries when I visited Père Lachaise in Paris since this was a big tourist spot. Therefore, it did not seem out of the ordinary to take a walk to see a castle-like mausoleum while going to one of the only places near downtown that is free of secondhand smoke, car exhaust, and trash and piss all over the walkways. After spending a couple hours here I called an Uber to get home. When the driver picked me up, he looked at me and with a sad tone asked "Is your family here?" I replied "No, I came here for fresh air." I did not bother to explain the polyps.

During May 2017 I flew from San Francisco to LA. The plane traveled over the lush Santa Cruz mountains just south of SFO. The sky was clear and the air looked clean. One hour later we were about to land at LAX and the entire county looked like it was covered in a thick film of gray smog for a hundred miles east from the ocean. It was time to leave this place. After I reached my two year mark I moved to the suburbs of Silicon Valley away from any urban core. The polyps and painful sneezing went away in a couple months. But I still wondered about the long term damage done by trying to live an environmentally friendly life in DTLA.

Ultimately, this lecture from life reinforced my belief that humans are consuming too much and degrading the environment. This strengthened my resolve to continue living an environmentally-friendly and simple life.

Chapter 38: Observing A Man Injecting Heroin And Issues Around Homelessness That Appear To Be Largely Ignored By Society

After pollution and traffic, the next most notorious issue in LA is homelessness. While I was not impacted in any substantially negative way, this challenge does pose issues that make living in DTLA taxing. The homeless situation is complex, so I did my best to accept this facet of life in LA.

About six months after moving to DTLA I headed over to the gentrifying Arts District. This newly hip area is adjacent to Skid Row, which has the highest concentration of homelessness in LA. During January 2016 I was at a food establishment specializing in slices of sweet pies. While in the restaurant I noticed a homeless woman wandering around. She lit a cigarette while inside. A young female employee tried to escort her out. The homeless woman did not want to leave nor did the worker lady want to touch the homeless person. So the employee picked up a chair and used it to slowly push out the homeless woman while avoiding physical contact. This was an emotional scene for the homeless woman, the employee, and the patrons. It made me feel sad about the homeless crisis.

Other times I was not sad. I was standing at an intersection in downtown and a young male asked me for money. Since I was asked for money every day, usually several times a day, I adopted a personal guideline of ignoring people asking for cash. This young lad was annoyed that I ignored him so he threatened to punch me. He created this scene during the daytime and in front of several other downtown working folk.

Another time I was walking back from Whole Foods in DTLA and a homeless woman touched my arm to get my attention. I kept walking. She walked after me yelling that I was a racist. She saw a homeless man in front of me waving a stick and yelled to him to hit me with his stick. I was tired of being asked for cash everyday. I would wear my work shirts and sweaters till I would get holes in the left elbow because my job required a lot of clicking of the mouse with my right hand but my left arm was free to sip warm beverages and eat snacks. And I would wear leather shoes and sneakers till they had holes. I was trying to pay off my debts and be fiscally responsible. For the first four months in LA I worked full time and studied an additional two hours a night and on weekends to obtain a license. These sacrifices kept me from handing out cash to everyone who asked. There are other ways to help homeless but I did not believe giving money to beggars on the street was the best way.

As DTLA neighborhoods like Little Tokyo were gentrifying, new residences were being built in areas that were once unsavory. Homeless people who lived in some of these areas were driven out. Several homeless individuals set up their living space in an alley about two hundred feet from my apartment. I did not mind homeless living in that alley, but I was troubled by changes that came along with these new neighbors. The folks living in the alley would dump their trash on the sidewalk near an electrical box and palm tree one hundred feet from my building. There would be piles of rubbish that amounted to several trash cans full. Since it was on the sidewalk the street sweeping vehicle did not clean it up. This de facto trash dump also became a bathroom. Foul aromas radiated from this unhygienic area. On a daily basis, I was forced to walk in the road as I passed this spot.

One day near this trash dump/outdoor bathroom site, I saw a homeless man convulsing on the ground. It appeared he was overdosing on drugs so I called emergency. During April 2017 I saw another homeless man who looked about my age curled up in a ball with three syringes on the ground next to him. The very next day there was yet another man shooting up drugs directly across the street from my apartment. He looked about fifty five years old. I was frozen in sadness as I stood behind the glass door and watched him heat up the drugs, put the poison into the needle, and inject himself on both sides of the abdomen. Then he walked back to the tent village in the alley. Little kids walked past him on their way home from the middle school a couple blocks away. A few days later a homeless woman was sitting on the curb about ten feet from my building and smoking a crack pipe.

Seeing that old man shooting up in front of my building in broad daylight was the first time I witnessed such activity in person. I got freaked out, especially because this was thirty feet from my residence. I called the local police station. I asked if they could come and search the tents. The officer said they would need a search warrant. I asked how this was possible if the tents were on public land. He mentioned that the liberals passed all these laws where this kind of situation is normal now and there is not much the police can do. He said possession of paraphernalia is only a misdemeanor and they can issue a citation at best since the drugs are probably gone by now. I told him I called 911 the day before because I saw a drug user who appeared to have overdosed and now I saw another shoot up in front of my building and close to a middle school. He said the police cannot go searching around because these homeless who use drugs have their rights protected by certain groups. I imagine this is more complicated than simplistically blaming liberals. Then I asked if he heard of drug users attacking local residents or if they usually keep to themselves. He asked me if I can fight. I stated that I did not want to fight anyone. He replied: If it comes down to it, you need to defend yourself.

I did not see this drug user as a criminal. Rather this was someone who was so down in life that they saw no other option than hard drugs. Even though this person was not a criminal, their actions could bring criminal elements to the community. Perhaps it is time that the US take a lesson from Portugal, which decriminalized small amounts of all drugs used for personal consumption, started treating addicts like victims rather than criminals, and developed infrastructure around rehabilitation and mental health. It could also help if the government invested more in programs that address root causes of drug abuse such as lack of education and health care as well as lack of focus on sense of community.

At least one city was trying to set an example. Around this time I read that Seattle was considering establishing the country's first safe injection site where addicts could inject inside, have access to clean needles, throw the needles out instead of onto the street where children walk, be near overdose medications, and be around addiction counselors so they could get help with recovery when they were ready. Unfortunately, such plans may not come to fruition if the state or federal governments get in the way of city initiatives. I began to fear for my safety because of used needles on the ground near my place, potential theft from addicts, an increase in drug dealers wandering around near my building, and the overall impact of this situation on my emotional well-being.

Tent villages and heaps of rubbish were all over downtown. This was too much to bear for someone who was growing more fond of nature while becoming less entertained by urban living. I got tired of smelling urine every time I walked anywhere. Eventually, I tried to convince myself that at least these folks were environmentally conscious since they did not waste much water to shower often or to flush the toilet. Perhaps the stench of urine all over was the sweet smell of environmentalism in action.

During October 2016 I was walking home from the Financial District. A gentle breeze was flowing eastward from the sea. An extremely foul aroma attacked my nasal passages. I looked ahead and saw a homeless man pushing a shopping cart full of cans. For nearly one hundred feet the wind carried the odor before the pungency reached my face. I wondered how society could provide shelter and showers for folks in need. I thought about what people living on the streets would do if recycling centers did not pay them for cans and bottles. My research led me to learn that California recycling centers are subsidized by the state. Apparently some subsidy payments vary depending on commodity prices. Lately more recycling centers have been closing down; especially in areas that were gentrifying. So, here we have an issue where the source of income for many homeless people as well as others who need extra pocket money is under threat. It will be interesting to see how governments attempt to address this issue.

During January 2017 I watched a Hazardous Materials truck, a dumpster truck, and three police cars drive into an alley in DTLA. I thought maybe there was some sort of toxic spill. It turns out, they were cleaning up a homeless encampment. It was strange that homeless villages were considered hazardous. I understood that many folks living on the street suffered from mental health conditions and could not operate within societal structures. So I did empathize, but at the same time, it was hard to deny that such transient individuals may create unsafe and possibly even harmful conditions for non-homeless people living in these areas.

Being around many struggling people everyday was emotionally difficult. One activity that helped me develop greater empathy and compassion for humans living in despair was finishing a book titled *Hunger* during November 2016. This novel published in 1890 by Norwegian Nobel Prize winner Knut Hamsun was about a man struggling to live on the streets of Norway. Since Knut Hamsun was instrumental to the literary technique known as stream of consciousness this book did a great job providing a look into the mind of a person living in desperate conditions.

My interest in American culture led me to this novel. In my twenties I started reading Hemingway books for fun because I related to his sense of adventure. Eventually I took a deeper interest in Hemingway's literary style and came across stream of consciousness. During my time in LA I also read *The Dharma Bums* by another stream of consciousness writer, Jack Kerouac. As I dug deeper into this technique I learned of Knut Hamsun. I wanted to research more about this writing style. I was not looking to learn about homelessness or develop empathy and compassion when I read the book, but I am grateful for the lesson. I strongly believe this short and easy read is a valuable resource for people living in urban environments with large homeless populations. In addition, I saw a film that did a tremendous job shedding light on homelessness and mental health issues. The 2009 film *The Soloist* starred Jamie Foxx as a homeless man living in DTLA. If even one more person can develop a greater sense of love for a fellow human who is struggling then, as a society, we may become one step closer to facing the challenges in front of us rather than ignoring them.

It is probably more practical to develop a sense of empathy and compassion for homeless people, and to one day possibly do a little part to help the situation, than it is to wait for a government to implement a viable long term solution. It seems that many issues around homelessness relate to the core tenets of American society. We are a country of winners and losers. Generally speaking, in America we believe in pulling ourselves up by our bootstraps rather than receiving "handouts." Unfortunately, we are also a nation that chooses to ignore how some of these social constructs can lead to mental health issues. As a society we seem to be preoccupied with building wealth and hastily moving forward than helping those in need. Our collective desire for more stuff has gotten to the point that our overworked culture has lost the ability to relax. On a deeper level, building the capacity for empathy and compassion is beneficial to even the most individualistic capitalist. One day almost everyone will experience a down period in their lives when they sink to the lowest lows. At this point, it will be beneficial to have developed the skill to treat humans gently - especially when the human that needs empathy and compassion is you yourself as you try to adopt kindness rather than harsh thoughts toward yourself to get back up.

Note: There are countless individuals in the greater LA area who are volunteering, working at non-profits, and pursuing their calling to help others through jobs with governments who are all working diligently to contribute what they can to help the homeless situation. While living in LA, I heard many stories about people doing their part to help homelessness. The fact that the homeless crisis continues to be severe is not meant to downplay the efforts of all those who are doing their best to help.

Chapter 39: Gang Graffiti On Government Vehicles

LA is also famous for ubiquitous graffiti. Almost weekly the local gang would spray paint their name on the building next to my apartment, my building, and even the sidewalk. Other times a rival gang would cross the spray paint out and put their own name over it. It was hilarious to see gang graffiti on the hood of a federal mail truck. Perhaps one day gangs will graffiti a police car too. But what was not funny is that trees - what few of them were downtown - were spray painted with graffiti. As an aspiring tree hugger, this made me lose some faith in humanity. I am unsure I have seen paint on trees anywhere other than in LA. Yet another reminder that this town was not for me. Even out on hikes an hour drive from downtown I sometimes saw trees that were completely covered in graffiti carved into the plant. The root of the issue here might be that LA is home to a surplus of artists who are yearning for the ability to express themselves creatively. If only the school systems had resources to provide mediums for artistic talent.

Chapter 40: Guardian Angels In The Sky Above Los Angeles

The amount of police activity around DTLA was astonishing. In January 2016 at around 11:30 a.m. I heard some commotion outside. I went on the roof of my apartment and saw twelve police vehicles two hundred feet from my apartment. A few months later in July 2016 there were nine police cars in front of my office building at 9:00 a.m. During October 2016 there was a small army of LAPD officers and their vehicles who shut down a city block. Apparently there was a murder in an apartment tower during the day.

Every few months I would see heavy duty military helicopters flying past downtown. And of course, each night when I was home, there was a police helicopter hovering over head about every hour. I wondered how in these modern times of drones in the military that the LAPD could still afford its massive fleet of helicopters with all their noise and exhaust pollution. My ears were exhausted from all this loud exhaust above.

Chapter 41: Showering With A Makeshift Bucket Of Cold Water

In exchange for saving about seven hundred bucks a month, the tradeoff was dealing with an old building. About once a month there would be no water for half a day while the pipes were being worked on. Apparently it was cheaper to put bandaids on than to address the root of the problem. I suppose that is common for a lot of issues in the world. While this was an annoyance it was probably worth the financial savings. This chapter of life was about temporary sacrifice anyway. In any case, one funny story came out of this water situation.

During October 2016 I flew to Oregon. On the morning of the flight I wanted to take a shower but the water was off. Oddly, the water was off in the shower but not in the sink next to it. I got a plastic gallon of water from the kitchen and cut it in half. Then I used the makeshift miniature bucket to fill it up and pour water on myself. But there was no hot water. So I was showering by a half gallon bucket of cold water at a time. This was worse than my winter in Ukraine where the place I was staying only had three minutes of hot water at a time. Some aspects of life in LA were of a lower standard of living than in the third world. But I actually embraced this experience because I never showered this way before. A part of me understood the value of moving toward discomfort rather than running away. It seemed prudent to practice embracing the bad in life because one day great suffering will arrive. Therefore, it may be beneficial to begin understanding that the full experience of life is much more than simply seeking pleasure and avoiding pain.

The cold shower did not end up mattering much because twelve hours later I was caught in a massive storm in Portland. By the time I arrived at a jazz club called Wilfs my pants were soaked all the way through. Perhaps the cold shower by bucket in LA was life's way to prepare me for the downpour later that day. The rain in Portland was so bad that night that the leader of the jazz group asked if anyone knew how to play piano because the pianist was caught in the storm. He eventually arrived forty minutes late.

Chapter 42: Seven Layer Dip

Traveling to many countries provided various lessons. One of which was that I grew tired of going to the most popular tourist sites in each place I visited. I yearned for something more than being surrounded by tourists taking photos. At this point, I wanted more "authentic" experiences like "locals" do. Eventually I thought about moving to some distant land and one day becoming a local. That is what I decided to try with Los Angeles. True, it was not a far away country near the equator. But there was an opportunity to have a deeper experience in one place where I never lived before. In addition, the city was rich with cultural amenities.

When settling down somewhere to get a more authentic experience, you eventually become well acquainted with the good, the bad, and the ugly. I define "settling down" in one location as moving somewhere, establishing some sort of semi-permanent residence, and actively seeking employment or a source of income. I did this in Puerto Rico where I lived for about two months. Then I got to experience a man pointing a gun to my chest. This was a truly authentic experience that a local might have unlike tourists at all inclusive beach resorts or cruise ship guests wandering around old San Juan. Several months later I spent two months in Ukraine. The country was experiencing a prolonged armed conflict on the border with Russia. One night I was at a live music venue chatting with local women. Then a soldier insisted I leave them so he could chat with the women. He advised he "needed it more than me" since he was involved in the armed conflict. Shortly thereafter he pulled a gun out and waved it in the air. Another authentic experience.

I learned that when you try to live somewhere you have a much richer and deeper experience than when simply visiting a locale. Vacations usually include a packed itinerary of tourism activities and splurging on restaurants. This is very different than actually living somewhere. When I was traveling around the world and rushing around a city for a few days or a week I only experienced the top layer of a seven layer dip. But this dish includes layers of beans, sour cream, guacamole, salsa, cheese, green onions, and olives or tomatoes. Conversely, when I lived in Puerto Rico and Ukraine for two months each, I experienced more layers. I even got to experience the layer of sour cream - a dairy product which has disgusted me since childhood and I do not eat till this day. Even in those two month periods I did not experience all seven layers of the dip.

Then I moved to LA and focused my energy exploring the city and surrounding areas. I got to experience all seven layers of the dip - even the sour cream pollution.

Two years of LA living taught me when the sour cream of life is served on your plate, it is better to accept it rather than push it away. To experience life is to take in all of it, not only the layers that give you pleasure. I can no longer eat only my favorite layer - the guacamole - of each dip I pass. Even the sour cream provides lessons and context that make the seven layer dip more rich and fulfilling. It is possible that one day I wake up and realize that sour cream has somehow become my favorite part of the dip of life. I have seen such evolutions and am learning to be more open to them. During my two years in Austin from 2012 to 2014 I had zero understanding why the city was obsessed with live music. Back then I thought live music was stupid. I believed an ideal evening out consisted of sitting at an establishment sipping a craft beverage and having a deep conversation. While I lived in Austin I went to a venue specifically for music only once. Fast forward a year or two after leaving Austin and I started to love live music so much that I would see shows monthly or sometimes weekly. A part of me woke up to the fact that sometimes it's better to listen to the world than to talk. Similarly, in my early teens I found it so bizarre that people actually watched old black and white movies or Westerns. I remember thinking my step-dad was strange because he liked Westerns. I wondered why anyone cared about events that happened several decades ago. A couple decades later, I find myself full of joy when I discover an entertaining classic film. Now it is interesting to see the history captured by moving pictures. I enjoy seeing how people spoke and treated each other in different eras. Classic films became a delightful way to see the progress of humanity. Therefore, I would not be surprised if a decade from now I become a connoisseur of artisanal sour creams.

The depth of my experience with the seven layer dip of LA showed me that I had so much abundance to be grateful for right in front of me.

Chapter 43: Efficiency And Conveniences Can Reduce Authenticity And Connection

One of the best foods I ate in LA while living there were grapes given to me by a woman I was dating. She got them from her father who grew a lot of his own food despite living close to DTLA. This was my first time experiencing homegrown grapes.

The small grapes were clustered so tightly and had thin sensitive skin unlike any store bought grape. Her father's grapes took more time to pick off their individual stems. Most of the time when you pulled one off the stem, a tiny portion of the stem stayed on the grape. This required the consumer to take that part off individually. Generally, such a two step process does not exist with store bought grapes bred for efficiency and convenience.

The taste and feel of these homegrown grapes were different than any from the supermarket. However, these grapes were more labor intensive to eat. You had to eat them shortly after they were cut off the vine. Otherwise, the weight of the tight cluster would squish the thin skin of other grapes underneath, causing them to spoil faster.

This experience with homegrown grapes reminded me that we live in a world where most goods are made to be efficient. However, commoditization can decrease the essence of goods and services. Many items we experience are not in their natural state. Now I had a fruit that was as close to its natural state as I have ever experienced with this variety of produce. Perhaps these less-efficient-to-eat, homegrown grapes are nature's way of reminding us to slow down in order to savor the moment. Perhaps when we slow down we can have an abundant experience with this fruit rather than scarfing down food as fuel for our momentum-filled day.

When society strives to make every aspect of living efficient and convenient, the citizens of that culture can begin to forget that life in its natural state is not always perfection created in a laboratory. There are aspects of life we may not like but which we need to accept. These inconvenient inefficiencies of the chaotic nature of world may be what we need in order to experience the full spectrum of life. Even if that means we have to eat one grape at a time and double up on the labor to pick hanging parts of stem from the grape.

Chapter 44: Almost All Of The Best Experiences Were Free Or Cost Very Little, The Role Of Connection To Other Humans, And Tuning Into The Abundance In Front Of Me

Living in LA from May 2015 to June 2017 was profound and positive. I grew a lot as a person. My goals of paying off my student loan and learning to love America were achieved. I also gained more wisdom than I expected.

I was able to leverage my knowledge from traveling to go on a world food tour within LA County. It was nice to learn more about the world without leaving a small geographic area. Since LA is home to many people of Mexican and Chinese ethnicity, I experienced regional specialities of cuisine from these countries. This was especially true when someone from a different ethnic background introduced me to a type of food I never heard of before.

There were countless delicious dishes that I tried during my time in LA. However, I was shown more gratitude when I cooked a savory meal for a companion than when I took a woman out and paid for a pricey restaurant bill. Similarly, I was most grateful when my experience with food involved the effort and love of someone close to me. I loved figs and was full of gratitude when fresh figs were in season. One day my boss brought in a dozen fresh figs from his yard, which were nicely packaged in a cardboard egg container. This was a delicious treat. The homegrown grapes from a girlfriend's father were also mouth watering. A coworker made a delicious cake from scratch and brought it in to share with us. The cake was made from graham crackers with layers of cream in between. Then the cake sat overnight so the crackers became soft and soggy. A secret ingredient dusted the top of the cake, which provided a hint of roastiness and slight bitterness to balance the light sweetness. During my travels I never tasted any food like this cake from a restaurant or store. The coworker was kind and you could tell the cake was made with loving intentions. Some of the culinary highlights from two years in LA were free. I enjoyed these experiences with food because I got to share them with people who were a big part of my waking life. This insight reinforced my belief that one does not need much to find joy in life. Yes, it is true that I enjoyed a delicious passion fruit cake at the famous and fancy dessert place in DTLA called Bottega Louie. But this ten dollar small individual serving cake was too sweet and too fancy. I would rather take the coworker's homemade creation. In addition, I loved when my boss introduced me to spicy cumin lamb from a far western province in China. This food became one of my favorite restaurant dishes for years. He also introduced me to a memorable rice porridge dessert with a hint of rice liquor inside. But I had a better time seeing the joy I brought a woman who, despite not liking lamb, deeply enjoyed my Uzbek plov. It was pleasant to see her surprise when she tried the rare combination of savory meat and sweet golden raisins. I appreciated this meal together much more than eating seafood at Gladstone's Restaurant located on the beach near Malibu. Furthermore, I enjoyed cooking my version of a deconstructed pizza for a date at home significantly more than going with a woman to a trendy deep dish pizza restaurant near hipster Silver Lake. I also enjoyed creating a funny dessert of corn on a stick covered in white chocolate and cinnamon and feasting on it together with a woman I was dating. The minimalist in me was inspired when I noticed a woman can be happier when you cook $5 worth of ingredients for her than other women who you wined and dined yet they took it for granted.

These experiences painted an interesting picture. It was better to make homemade food with loved ones than dine at fancy restaurants. This was a valuable lesson which motivated me to focus my time on nourishment that brought joy rather than lusting for fancy feasts to satisfy ego more than belly. If I lost all the memories stored on my smartphone, the food experiences I would remember most are those that I shared with people who meant a lot to me and that involved food that was prepared with love.

When there is an intention of love in the food, another human thought about you when they made the food. Mortal beings have a limited time in our bodies. We want to be remembered. We want to be loved, or at least thought about. No one remembers you when you go to a restaurant. The people preparing your food will never see who you are. It is for these reasons that some of the best foods I tried in LA were those that were given to me with me in mind. Furthermore, some of the tastiest cuisine I ate during the LA years were actually when I went home to San Diego and feasted with family on schnitzel made from scratch, Russian vinaigrette salad, and homemade pierogies. This family feast came with a homemade cake consisting of a dozen layers of crepes with cream between each and was garnished with dark chocolate shavings on top. The crepe cake tasted unlike any dessert I ate at a restaurant. Other soul fulfilling dishes were with different family members who often prepared delicious and wholesome fish cooked in various styles. It was comforting to come home and be greeted with comfort food made with love.

Aside from culinary experiences, my time in LA was full of learning about the arts, culture, and history that made America great. Much like my encounters with food, the experiences that were most memorable were extremely budget-friendly. Most cultural amenities that I enjoyed were in the neighborhood of twenty dollars. Sure, I did love on one occasion to experience excellent seats at the Walt Disney Concert Hall while the orchestra played the music to the film. However, many of my fondest memories were free. I still recall the pleasant night that I started falling in love with jazz as a brass player slid across the floor on his back and the drummer went around drumming people's cups. That event changed my life. It made living in America all the more enjoyable, and encouraged me to continue going to live jazz often. Another great memory from that night was the scent of bergamot oil on the neck of my date. I have been on many dates and smelled many different, and oftentimes expensive, perfumes but I remember this Earl Grey scent the most. This aroma was on the body of a woman who was also living a budget-minded life. Another long standing memory was when I watched a street musician play the sax, engaged in a lengthy chat with him, and was informed about The Baked Potato. That encounter led to experiencing passion-fueled funk in a tiny venue while feeling one with the music.

Life kept finding a way to show me that there was so much goodness available in front of me that cost very little. I just needed time to tune into it and appreciate it.

Supporting arts and music was like voting with my dollars for a good cause. The proceeds from my visits to museums and shows helped continue artistic endeavors by fellow citizens. Furthermore, being a patron of the arts allowed me to purchase knowledge and experiences that would continue to grow and add value to my life rather than buying more material possessions which generally decline in value over time. After having many delightful experiences at museums and music shows, I felt a deeper understanding of the human need for creative expression and the desire to convey one's interpretation of life. More importantly, I would often walk away from an art museum or a live music show feeling a more profound sense of understanding that art is about the triumph of the human spirit and all of the challenges that we overcome as a species.

These insights led me to believe that spending on arts in various forms supports the progress of society. This is especially true when there is a big push for successful careers in science, technology, engineering, and math in a society on a quest to make goods and services more convenient and efficient. We need artistic folks and people with sensitive minds who will ponder and contemplate how all these technological changes and innovations affect the human psyche. As society becomes more scientific and less religious it is important to have poems such as those by Walt Whitman which can help make sense of existence and death in ways that science cannot.

The knowledge I gained about America provided a better foundation for lifelong learning. It made life more abundant because I can find joy in the little things that I pass by or hear about on a daily basis. Learning provided context which helped develop gratitude toward everyday occurrences in any town or city - not just LA.

I also recognize that some of the most special moments were when someone took the time to be kind - even if the gesture was small. We humans want to feel like we made a positive impact on someone's life, which can happen when people treat us well and vice versa.

Perhaps some of the best experiences I had in LA over those two years were the simple ones and those with people who meant a lot to me. A woman took the time to draw me an artistic picture of a microwave because I did not have my own such appliance. A coworker took the time to handwrite a heartfelt note thanking me for being me. A boss treated me to an authentic meal from his culture on his own dime. A supervisor gave me their respect and trust after I completed a challenging project on my own. Even my apartment manager who lived in the building was always jovial and was definitely the best apartment manager I encountered. The dentist was equally as cheerful and funny and full of knowledge about jazz and travel. This was the only time I enjoyed visiting the dentist - and I actually saw him quite a few times. Having that light bulb moment after wandering around the Norton Simon Museum and thoughts finally clicking - over the past few centuries art is a record of the evolution of the human mind. Finally seeing that the more I learned about culture and the arts, the more context I had to value other aspects of life. All this humanities knowledge was building on itself and exposing th interconnectedness of the world. Contemplating a still li painting of fruit from centuries ago that looks much differ than our current varieties altered for mass consumption. Being introduced by a woman to her world of cinema and beginning to love that passion of hers as much as she does. Feeling grateful because your desire to learn about America was attracting people into your life for this reason. Reaching optimal health, mental clarity, and calm because I was finally able to respect myself and eat with my stomach rather than my mind. Finally understanding that overeating can result when the mind is preoccupied by stress or anxiousness. And learning that sometimes we eat unnecessarily because of a craving as a result of a fond memory rather than hunger. When both sisters came to visit after I lived in LA for a year and a half, I was able to take them to my favorite spots including the Huntington Garden, my go-to hike, and the Armenian business near Thai Town that sells fresh pressed raw sugar cane juice. My boss getting me my favorite store bought cake - Red Velvet from Nothing Bundt Cakes. After two years of studying America, I finally learned to accept, appreciate, and love the country where I was residing rather than always looking beyond our borders for great experiences.

It is the people who treat you with care and respect that make it all worthwhile. And my encounters with all the wonderful folks I met in LA have inspired me to be a kinder and gentler human.

Chapter 45: The Relationship Between Jazz And The Meaning Of Life, From Letting Go Of Material Objects To Letting Go Of Non-Material Things, And The Acceptance Of Painful Life Events As A Catalyst For Deeper Experiences

One lesson I learned from jazz is that I do not know the meaning of jazz. Three years after I fell in love with this music I cannot definitively explain what it is. I have zero formal music education and have never even taken a course or read a book on music or its theory. So I do not know what jazz is in technical terms. But I do not need to know what jazz is to love it, be completely absorbed by it, and to fully experience it. In this sense, jazz is like life. Sometimes it is better to not fuss about definitions, meaning, and to overthink ideas. Sometimes it is better to surrender to the experience in all its good, bad, and ugly saliva splattering from the trumpet onto the stage.

Similarly, I have little idea about the meaning of life. But I did not need many possessions or deep pockets to experience the richness and depth of life. What I needed was a simple life with few bills and few desires so I could have more time to focus on the simple joys in front of me. Such values include personal growth, lifelong learning, spending time in nature, exercise, and seeking nutrition from food prepared with good intentions.

I met many wealthy individuals throughout the US over the course of my career in financial services. I have been in their offices, homes, and enjoyed meals with them at restaurants. Some of them shared personal details. Even wealthy people faced hardship at various points in their life. Even rich people die. All people, regardless of wealth, will have to muster the courage to face the final adventure. I wondered if people believed that having wealth and possessions helped them feel more secure about our mortality. Then I began contemplating why many are insecure about our fate in a world that is constantly changing. It made little sense to deny that life is full of sunsets and winters which remind us that we will be in the ground one day, regardless of bank account size.

These experiences inspired me to appreciate the abundance in front of me in the present rather than habitually delaying gratitude till some point in the future. There was little need to delay joy till a goal was accomplished, a better job title was achieved, a higher salary was earned, or one could finally afford a luxury vacation. If we lost all our wealth and closest family members, we would need to find some joy to get us out of bed and bring a smile to our faces. The human spirit would need to triumph. There will come a time in everyone's life when they wake up and find they have an itch that they cannot scratch. No amount of surplus wealth can make the itch go away. We finally realize that life is more than limiting pain and seeking pleasure. The only choice is to accept and move forward with our values.

I thought that if I could live with minimal possessions, residential space, without a car, and without debt then life would be ok. As it turns out, the adventure into minimalism was just a foundation. The next advancement required letting go of attachments to unnecessary emotions, thoughts, mental states, and even people that I once loved. Such attachments are more difficult to let go of than microwaves and personal automobile ownership.

One non-material attachment I let go of in LA was my youth. After thirty years of nearly perfect health I finally experienced that my health would start to decline. At this point I realized that the good, the bad, and the ugly in life can be a catalyst for positive experiences with the right perspective. I began to believe that each curveball that life throws at you - even those that cause pain and suffering - come with a silver lining. We do not need more assets to see how a terrible situation can lead to positive outcomes. Instead, we need emotional intelligence. And to gain more of this we need time. We need time to read, to meditate, to exercise, to eat healthy, to practice mindfulness, to practice gratitude, to try to be involved with a community, and to have a creative outlet. We need time to see that the detours life takes us on are not actually detours but are gifts. Abundance can be found in even the most agonizing circumstances that come our way when we stop running away from pain and fear. Instead it is beneficial to accept that suffering is part of the plan for our continued evolution in an ever changing, chaotic world. One day we'll look back on the struggle and see how it was necessary to teach us what we needed to know.

Letting go of attachments to possessions and starting my journey to learn to let go of non-material things should not be seen as losing something per se. Instead, letting go is gaining something. When we let go, we gain the ability to adapt. And adaptability is one of the primary skills for survival.

Accepting that pain and suffering could bring insight about adaptability allowed me to see that this pilgrimage into my mind would continue to change over time. I could wake up tomorrow and learn that I have developed an allergy to one of my most beloved foods - the dozen varieties of nuts I snack on weekly. Instead of going nuts, I am in a better place to accept this and learn to love some new aspect of life and continue to change with the world.

Each of us has our own journey. Instead of taking any one person's advice about what path to embark on to improve our health or any other situation we need to dedicate time to think clearly about our own body and mind. We need to prioritize tuning into ourselves and starting the trial and error process to find what works and what does not. Starting to seek answers is a step in the right direction.

When you make time to work on body, mind, and spirit you notice that time is one of the most precious gifts on earth. When you have an afternoon to spend on a long hike in the wilderness without cell phone reception you see the bountiful joy in nature. You notice the impact that such a trek in the woods can have on easing the mind and spirit. Dedicating time to simple tasks such as eating a fig can be the difference between savoring every morsel, and being enamored with the world for producing such divine delicacies, or it can be an experience where you scarf down the fruit without consciously processing what is happening while you see the food as fuel for your march toward a future goal. With dedicated time even the most simple act can be a profound experience. One of the best strategies to find more time is to simplify life.

In addition to providing more time, a simple life can allow greater flexibility. I noticed that when I paid off my debt, built up a safety cushion, and learned to live small I was less worried about potentially losing my job. In turn, this allowed me to be more productive. Instead of needing a promotion because I decided to move to a fancier residence, I did not feel that I was overthinking situations at work and putting unnecessary stress on myself. I was able to take on new challenges for the sake of growth in and of itself without much concern for potential increase in money or title that may not come. In turn, I believe this made me a better employee.

If I wanted to change careers or desired to strive for a non-traditional pursuit, I wanted to be in a position to pursue my calling without worrying about maintaining a fancy lifestyle. There might be a time in the future where I want to take a job because I love the work more than I love the pay. If such a time ever comes, I want to be in a good position to pursue my dreams. Ultimately, I found it is better to need little than to be able to afford a lot.

Chapter 46: Society's Formula: Work Towards X And When You Achieve It You Will Be Happy, The Faultiness Behind This Equation, Believing X Would Be Better 'IF' Y, Having Enough, Living Out Values Instead Of Goals, And The Impact Of These Changes On Our Relationships With People

Life led me down a path where I saw that our society largely adopted the following formula: Work towards some goal, then when you achieve it, you will be happy. Somewhere along the way, some logic in this equation broke down and many people got into a vicious cycle. Once people achieved the possessions or salary they thought would bring them happiness they were unsatisfied and needed more. As a creature of habit, the mind can start to equate the future with happiness.[1] Many people have gotten trapped in a cycle of enough is never enough. Large portions of the population believe that we need more to finally be happy. I have been guilty of this countless times, especially as it relates to travel and adventure experiences. I would be in the middle of a trip and start looking up information about the next adventure before the one in the moment was finished.

I am embarking on a journey where I actively strive to believe that I have enough. This is a radical paradigm shift compared to how I lived most of my life. I thought if I had more money I would be happier. I thought if I could go on more international adventures I would be happier. I thought that if certain family members treated me better I would be happier. I thought if a supervisor was a bit gentler I would be happier. I would feel more handsome if my nose was smaller. I would feel sexier if certain parts of my body were symmetrical. I would be happier if I was more successful because then some of my family members would be proud that I became an immigrant rags-to-riches story. I got stuck on the following formula: This relationship / event / job / meal / etc... would be better *if* [insert condition]. Now I am willing to accept that things are how they are and to find joy in the present moment and in each day. Sure, if a relationship or supervisor or environment or anything else is causing you so much stress that you start developing physical symptoms, you may want to get out quickly. There is a difference between some discomfort that one can endure in order to grow and experience life for what it is, compared to unnecessary pain that we can stop if we let go of mental attachments to whatever got us into a situation in the first place.

This is by no means advocacy of laziness, giving up, or for anyone to stop challenging themselves. I will continue to strive to evolve as a human in an ever changing world. I will continue working on the ability to adapt to life as it comes. I will continue finding joy in finishing a book as well as all other forms of lifelong learning. I choose to believe that I, as well as many other humans, have an innate desire to create quality work and collaborate on projects that help society progress. Humans are able to derive more joy along these journeys when they are not repeatedly told they are not enough by themselves or others. Conversely, I no longer choose to believe that I can only be content after reaching some goal I set for myself before life changed so much that the initial goal actually makes little sense. I might reach a different milestone than the one I set for myself years before. I now see that the chaotic world will continue to change constantly so it is okay to adapt goals often. And I also see that it is crucial to find joy in the abundant balls of delight that we encounter each day instead of being so rigid that we need to complete some endeavor before we allow ourselves to appreciate the present moment.

When we choose to believe that we have enough we notice that not everything needs to be improved all the time. This is especially true for those events that we have zero control over. When we start thinking that enough is enough in terms of possessions, money, titles, and bigger houses, we notice that the assumption that more improvement leads to happiness is not necessarily accurate. At this point, we begin to treat people differently. With mindfulness you think twice before offering unsolicited advice to your friend on how they can improve their situation. You pause for a moment to think before making demands of friends or significant others. You notice that by constantly looking for areas of improvement you overlook the positives. Then you see that sometimes it is better to say nothing than it is to point out a way that a particular situation or thing would be better "*if*."

If people are constantly telling you that you are not doing enough and are not meeting their insatiable expectations, then perhaps they are not ready to accept you as you are. Some people with this mindset may never be satisfied. There is a difference between thinking that my relationship with someone would be better if this person demanded a little less compared to mindfully recognizing that I may be in a potentially harmful environment. As we learn to respect ourselves we learn to tell the difference between these two scenarios. Then we can choose to part ways with people whose attitude prevents them from finding contentment in their heart. In my humble opinion, many health issues of the body and the mind come from the belief that what we have available to us in the present is not enough. I choose to start believing that I have enough. I simply need time, tranquility, and the right mindset to see how much abundance is already in front of me.

Acknowledgments

With deep gratitude I want to acknowledge the people who helped with this book.

Steve Frost has been a great friend over the years. He also dedicated many hours to edit the book and provided strategic direction. His advice was invaluable. More importantly, he helped me stay focused throughout the many setbacks that come along with such an undertaking. I am most grateful for his encouragement and infectious positivity. Some of his ideas even found their way into the book. Back when I lived in Texas I once asked him what he thought the meaning of life was. He replied that the meaning of life is not asking such questions. What he meant was that life is meant to be experienced not over-analyzed. I did not understand the lesson back then as deeply as I do now.

The book could not have been brought into its current state without the help of my long time friend Contessa Semaan.

She has been a tremendous friend over the past decade. So when she offered to take a look at my manuscript, I could not refuse such a kind offer. Furthermore, she attended the University of Southern California, lived in LA, and has a wealth of experience in business writing. Before she started editing I asked her to focus on grammar because I was fatigued from writing and rewriting this book for several months. Fortunately, she found many other opportunities for improvement than simply more grammar edits. Her vision for the project provided many excellent points with which I could not disagree. I am glad she pushed me to make the final product even better.

My friend Eric Klingermier from college contributed to this book without even knowing it. His friendship has provided me with many valuable insights. His background in psychology has allowed me to learn a lot about the mind from our many discussions over the years. Even in June 2017 we discussed acceptance and suffering as well as letting go of non-material attachments such as negative thoughts, states of mind, and emotions. And more recently he helped me better understand concepts such as re-framing and emotional resilience. He has always been very encouraging in my pursuit of minimalism - in both the material and non-material sense.

After an impromptu trip to Portugal during December 2018 I came back eager to learn about mindfulness. I was familiar with the topic for years from various articles and occasional attempts at meditation. But I wanted to know more.

So I started reading books related to mindfulness after that trip. Then I moved back to my hometown of San Diego in January 2019 and started going to yoga almost everyday. The studio was locally owned and the instructors seemed more philosophical than those who worked at national chain gyms or YMCA where I previously tried yoga. By this point I was asking a lot of questions and spending significant time reflecting and contemplating. Simultaneously I was writing the second half of this book. During this time a book found me at just the right time that I needed it. I started reading *The Wisdom of Insecurity* by Alan Watts (New York. Second Vintage Books Edition. 2011) around February 2019. This book had a profound impact on me. Many of the thoughts I had over the years were already said - and done so in such an eloquent and concise fashion in his book.

In addition, during my pursuit of gaining a greater understanding of mindfulness I came across Acceptance and Commitment Therapy (ACT). This psychological approach uses mindfulness to help people attain the lives they want to live. As I was learning about ACT I noticed many of the topics covered were also being discussed in yoga class. Then I noticed points made by *The Wisdom of Insecurity* were also brought up during yoga. Many of these ideas were concepts that I thought about and discussed with people as I began my first major transformation in life. It felt serendipitous that all these worlds came together at the same time. I felt that the energy I was sending out into the world brought answers to me. I just needed to start seeking answers. And, here I would like to thank the yoga instructors at my local yoga studio in San Diego, who let me pick their brains after class. I was surprised that all the ideas I sought for years were known by so many people. I felt grateful that so much of what I yearned to know was readily available. As I was undergoing a several month long transformation, while simultaneously working on this book, there were several yoga instructors whose kindness and encouragement indirectly contributed to this book.

I am the kind of person that likes to connect the dots. As such, I ask a lot of questions. Perhaps people who know me know this about me. With this in mind, I want to thank everyone else who entertained my questions and who helped me work out the many ideas found in this book. Of course, the contents in this book are my interpretations of what I have learned and not necessarily a representation of any person's views.

I also want to show my appreciation for all the people I met in Los Angeles during my two years there. They made my time in the city memorable. This was especially true of my colleagues at work. Of course, I am also grateful for meeting Lillia Salazar who introduced me to the world of cinema and with whom I shared many LA adventures.

Last but not least, I want to thank the members of my family, friends, and colleagues who encouraged me to pursue this project.